I0223289

Magnetic:

How Anyone Can Learn Genuine Charisma, Confidence, Body Language, & People Reading Skills Without Being Weird, Needy

Or Arrogant (2 in 1 Bundle)

© Copyright Darcy Carter 2019 - All rights reserved.

The contents of this book may not be reproduced, duplicated or transmitted without direct written permission from the author.

Under no circumstances will any legal responsibility or blame be held against the publisher for any reparation, damages, or monetary loss due to the information herein, either directly or indirectly.

Legal Notice:

You cannot amend, distribute, sell, use, quote or paraphrase any part or the content within this book without the consent of the author.

Disclaimer Notice:

Please note the information contained within this document is for educational and entertainment purposes only. No warranties of any kind are expressed or implied. Readers acknowledge that the author is not engaging in the rendering of legal, financial, medical or professional advice. Please consult a licensed professional before attempting any techniques outlined in this book.

By reading this document, the reader agrees that under no circumstances are is the author responsible for any losses, direct or indirect, which are incurred as a result of the use of information contained within this document, including, but not limited to, —errors, omissions, or inaccuracies.

Buyer Bonus:

Rituals Of The Rich & Famous

Free Access to Success Tips, Strategies and Habits of The Rich & Famous

Join successful subscribers!

Get 4 new strategies every week on how to be more charismatic, confident, and happy.

<u>Free Sign Up Here</u>

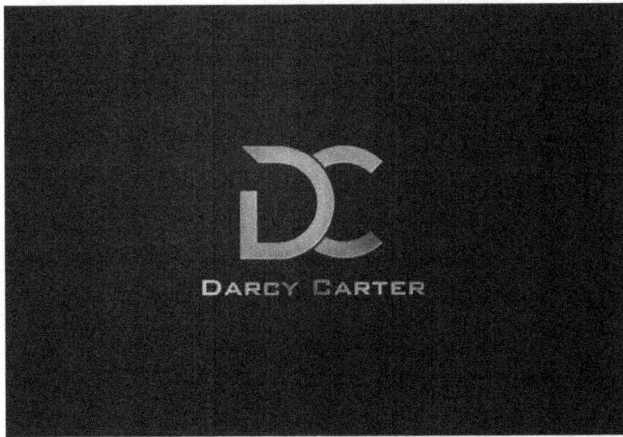

<u>Buyer Bonus 2</u>

<u>Attachment Theory, The Science of Successful Relationships, Authentic Love, Romance and Connection</u>

Discover the secrets to building healthy, happy, and rewarding relationships.

The key ingredient to happy and fulfilled people is the quality of their intimate, social, family, and professional relationships - nothing else in life comes even remotely close.

Go ahead, transform the quality of your relationships and make love work for you.

ATTACHMENT THEORY

The Science of Successful Relationships, Authentic Love, Romance and Connection

DARCY CARTER

Charisma:

7 Ways to Develop Genuine Charisma, Social Skills & Increase Your Confidence

Contents

Introduction

Charisma is seen as a key aspect of a great personality.

The ability to delight and charm other people - to be funny, to be interesting, to be disarming - is a valuable trait that you can develop and will help you in your personal and business relationships.

Perhaps you have learned from "personality gurus" that you can fake charisma using certain strategies used by celebrities, leaders, and keynote speakers. But unfortunately, this is far from the truth.

Enhancing your charisma doesn't mean you need to be always happy or making everything bright and perky. In fact, there are situations that you may need to do the opposite.

Improving your likability is about exploring what is genuinely likable in you, in the people around you, and in your relationships. It is via the strength of authenticity that valuable networks can become meaningful relationships.

For you to boost your charisma, you need to understand its nature and dynamics. We have our unique personalities, which makes it really exciting to explore the social sphere. We have our own charisma, but still, the fundamental drivers of likability are the same for everyone.

In this book, we will take a closer look at specific ways that can help you improve your likability in both personal and business settings:

- *Authenticity*
- *Self-Perception*
- *Energy*
- *Curiosity*
- *Similarities and Differences*
- *Value*
- *Mood Memory*

These methods for connecting with people you like will provide you to grab more opportunities and nurture your social life. By studying these methods, you will discover what is naturally likable about yourself, and how you can share these qualities with the people you meet to build relationships that are genuine.

By enhancing your charisma, you can help yourself to be more successful, more comfortable, and be generally happier.

Once again, thanks for downloading this book, I hope you find it to be helpful!

Chapter 1 - Be Authentic

How exactly can a person be more authentic?

The specifics can be different for each of us because we all have different values, goals, knowledge, skill sets, beliefs, behaviors, and attitudes. But in a general sense, authenticity is the same for all of us. Authenticity invokes being natural that when you are true to yourself, you might not even notice it.

On the other hand, you will easily notice when you are not your natural self. You are not comfortable, you feel awkward, maybe stressed and unconfident, and usually after spending a significant amount of time where you are really just faking it, you feel drained - not just tired.

There's a difference between drained and tired.

Being tired is physically manifested but being drained involves mental exhaustion. This feeling of emptiness comes from the emotional or mental effort of exerting energy so you can act in a manner that is really not natural for you.

You can be drained if you are doing something that doesn't really feel right. What is really happening inside your mind when you are not being your true self?

Perhaps, you really don't like socializing at a party, but you are just trying to be polite. Or maybe you don't like a particular person, but you are trying to act cordial.

Some people feel drained all the time because they are forced to act like a successful communicator. They believe that they are not likable if people cannot respond positively to them. Some are really not comfortable in a particular situation and they just don't know what to do.

Most of these reasons really represent things that you feel you are expected to do, or you feel that you are vulnerable. You may put on a mask when, for any reason, you feel you are not up to something or you just dread a specific situation.

Being authentic is not only a particular method to be charismatic, but it is also the overarching theme of this book.

As you read through this book, you will learn that being genuine is a basic element in other ways to enhance your social skills. It is key to charisma because it captures the essence of being likable. Your authentic self is your best self. You will discover that authenticity is a powerful tool in forging genuine relationships with the people you want to attract.

When Are You Authentic?

In order to identify the specific situations when you can really say that you are authentic, you should explicitly focus on how you feel at the start of a new connection and how you feel at the end.

If you dread a situation, pause and identify what it triggers that uncomfortable feeling. Is it the environment, the task, or the person? If you really like a situation, pause and try to identify what makes you feel comfortable?

Take note of your responses and try to take a closer look at each one. Your responses must disclose important details about the types of experiences that trigger you to shy away from presenting your authentic self as well as those experiences that you feel find it easier to be authentic.

Leverage these self-images about what you naturally feel and consider them as your home base perception where you can return from time to time to really understand what authenticity means for you.

How to Be Authentic?

Being authentic means presenting who you are - your natural energy and your genuine responses.

Sharing what is authentic about you is the cornerstone of building real connections with other people. Whenever you present your authenticity, people will also respond naturally. This establishes the bedrock for growth, connections, and mutual understanding.

But how can you become authentic?

The great thing about becoming authentic is that it doesn't require a lot of effort. You don't need to go the extra mile because you just need to be.

Yes, it is easy to be authentic, but embracing this principle can be easier said than done.

With our hectic schedules, many of us tend to just hustle through situations without spending too much thought, and so we may not even be conscious when we are and are not being authentic.

Even if we are aware that we are not authentic (whenever we are putting on a mask or just sleepwalking through a situation) it is often not easy to interfere with the behavior.

However, the key is to just stop trying to be who you think you must be and stop premeditating or monitoring your actions. Just be your true self.

Have you ever wondered why reality shows are now such big hits on television? Popular reality shows such as "America's Next Top Model" or "Big Brother" have garnered millions of eyeballs around the world and continue to rake in millions of dollars in revenue.

One reason is that people are just tired of scripted shows and they want to take a peek into the real living situations of models vying to take the next spot in the limelight or witnessing some crazy scenarios involving strangers who are now spending 24/7 with each other inside a house.

So many of these shows will allow you to see primal struggles between personality types, and it can be fascinating to see the dramas play out.

Have you seen how kids behave without any filter? They naturally shine when they are in their authentic selves. While you don't need to be child like, you can use this home base to reconnect with that uncensored experience of being a kid, before adulthood began changing you based on what it perceived to be the bigger world you wanted.

Just try to think back to the time that preceded adult responsibilities and worries to a time when your behaviors, intentions, and emotions were largely unfettered.

Once you are able to establish this primal connection, you can feel at ease. You will soon realize that even though you might dread being part of a large crowd and you are compelled to be the life of the party; you can be totally comfortable in engaging small groups or one-on-one.

Under these controlled settings, you may easily engage people in more meaningful conversations about the things that really matter to you most.

The Test for Authenticity

Whenever you are in a situation that makes you feel disconnected or uncomfortable, step back and take a closer look if you are being authentic.

If you can say that you are authentic, then sure, continue doing what you are doing. There are instances that being uncomfortable or disconnected could mean that you have to refocus your attention so you can reconnect with the situation with more authenticity.

The discomfort you feel in a particular situation might be caused by pushing yourself affirmatively. Under such circumstances, the discomfort might be part of being genuine.

However, if you believe that you are not authentic in that situation, then you might need to dig deeper to know the deeper reason behind the discomfort or disconnect.

Probably you might be changing your behavior because of how you think you must act. Moreover, there might be something about the situation, which makes you a bit nervous or lacking.

For such scenarios, try to relax and reconnect with that aspect of you that you feel genuine and honest.

Try visualizing the worst case scenario. You will discover that usually, the outcome is not all that bad. Just anchor on your contribution to the situation. Presenting your authentic self will help you in establishing your connection regardless of the result.

Activity: Reframing Authenticity

You can present your authentic self whenever you make the choices you want to make and not just the ones that you think you should really make.

It's not only about choosing the situations that you want to be part of but deciding how you want to respond to the events as they happen.

You can bring four basic colors to categorize each behavior that you can any situation. This will help reaffirm what is genuine for yourself or help you readjust your approach so you can reveal your authentic self.

Red

The color red pertains to what the community, your company, or some other external forces think what you should do. While you may agree with some of them, these are the things that you wouldn't want to do, but rather what you feel you are obliged to do.

Orange

This refers to the things you really dread, although you understand the importance of accomplishing them.

Green

This refers to the things that you really want to do, although choosing and doing them is often difficult for you.

Blue

This refers to the things that make you really excited, alert, and genuinely giddy.

As a quick assessment, select anything from your daily tasks or your calendar of activities, and then promptly, without too much thinking, select the right color that is most appropriate for each task.

You might be surprised by how much this basic exercise will reveal. For example, if you have an upcoming presentation with an important client, you could find yourself thinking that you have to persuade the boss of a big corporation, or you have to persuade a client that can save your business.

Notice that even if you need to deal with the same situation, you can change your perception towards it. Same situation, different attitudes. Once you determine what your attitude is, you can consider your options and decide what to do about it.

Your first option is to pursue the activity if you tagged as blue or green because it will become effortless for you. If you tagged the pitch as orange or red then you have to determine how to get over it if the task is crucial even if the authentic desire to do it is not really present. In these scenarios, find a way to complete the task that will allow you to be genuine with yourself.

Chances are, your job entails attending meetings and mingling with clients and coworkers. This might be a key part of your job regardless of how uncomfortable it is for you.

But instead of imposing an inauthentic role on yourself or trying to be the life of the party, you can instead choose to talk with smaller groups, that can make you more effective and comfortable. You can still do things that you dread but are important without compromising your authenticity.

Another option is to reframe your mindset. There are instances that it is powerful and possible to approach a situation from a new perspective, which could literally change the way you perceive it.

For example, if your original attitude towards a client pitch was "I have to attend a pitch and persuade this client," you can reframe it by saying "I want to share our service that can really help this client increase his sales."

By reframing a challenging situation, you can focus on the characteristics of it that can make you feel energized and good. With this, you can recast the activity as green or blue.

There are instances that you don't have any option left but to avoid the situation. But take note that it is not always easy to just let go of an activity. There are certain activities that should be completed, and in these activities, you have to put on your best effort.

Before you let go of activities that you have tagged as red or orange, it pays well if you take a second look at them. Sometimes, people have a tendency to be deeply ingrained in the red or orange mentality that it could dominate our thinking and really cloud our judgement to the point where we might just give up.

However, if you think that a red or orange activity is not really important, and that completing it is just for compliance, then let it go. If you are not capable of working on the task with your full energy and authenticity, then you may not make the best use of your time or yourself.

Common Bad Habits that Make People Instantly Dislike You

The first impression really lasts, and it may not take more than three minutes to make someone realize that they don't want to spend time with you.

Many of the ways that turn people off are caused by lack of authenticity such as the following:

Hiding Your Real Emotions

Studies show that showing your genuine emotions is a better way to get people like you than hiding them inside.

For example, in one study, researchers videotaped the reactions of people watching a sad scene in the film "The Champ" and the fake orgasm scene in the film "When Harry Met Sally".

In some scenes, the actors were told to naturally react, and in another, they were told to bottle up their emotions. The researchers then presented the four versions of the videos to some college students and measured how much they are interested in befriending the people in the videos.

Results showed that those who suppressed their emotions were perceived as less charismatic compared to people who have shown their natural emotions.

Telling Secrets to Strangers

Basically, people become more close to each other if they share secrets. As a matter of fact, self-disclosure is one of the best ways to befriend someone.

However, scientists reveal that disclosing something that is too personal such as your cousin having an affair can significantly decrease your likability because you may be perceived as insecure.

There is no need to share intimate secrets to a person whom you really want to be close with. If you are in the early stages of a relationship, you can just share details about your hobbies or your favorite memories. This will make you more likable.

Being Overly Nice

You may think that you can win people over by becoming too nice, but research suggests otherwise.

In a study conducted at Washington State University in 2010, researchers provided college students with points that they may keep or exchange for meal vouchers.

The participants were oriented that they were playing in five groups, although the other four groups were accomplices who were ordered by the researchers to be overly nice. The actual participants were told that giving up their points would increase the chances of the group to receive cash rewards.

Other fake participants were instructed to give away lots of points and insisted on taking a few meal vouchers. After the activity, most participants said they were not interested to work with their teammates who were unselfish. They thought that the participants who were overly nice had ulterior motives.

So you may think twice about always volunteering to fix the printer or get the pizza. Sometimes, you have to say no but be sure to explain why you can't extend a hand.

Humblebragging

Humblebragging is the act of criticizing yourself, but actually you are really complimenting. This can turn-off not only your friends but also potential employers.

In one study, researchers asked college students to write down their biggest weakness in the workplace. Results indicated that around 75% of participants answered: "working too hard" or being "perfectionist".

However, independent research assistants said they like the participants who were honest and would be open to hiring them. The responses of the participants were like "there are times that I find myself overreacting" and "It is not easy for me to be organized at work".

To make sure that you ace that classic job interview question, you can talk about your weakness that is not directly related to the job - for instance, a fear of selling to people if you're applying for a video editor position.

Introverted Authenticity

Many introverts think that building relationships and forging connections come easily with extroverts. Most extroverts cannot confirm or deny this as they usually don't think too much about it as they are quite busy being genuine that they often ignore the need to pause and assess what they are doing.

But as a matter of fact, extroverts also face their own challenges when it comes to building relationships as you will later learn in this book.

If you are an introvert, you should know that you can still be comfortable in social and business situations. Being introverted doesn't mean you are weak.

More often than not, introverts are naturally capable of initiating connections because they have great listening skills.

If you are introverted, it is important for you to listen to your own rhythms and don't worry about sounding like your extroverted friends. Focus on the things that you are most comfortable doing. For instance, if you're exhausted, you can simply leave a gathering or a party so you can rest. You don't have to "go with what your friends would want you to do".

When you are with a group of people, do you opt to be a listener and speak only when you have something important to share? There is nothing wrong with doing just that. When it comes to attitudes, you should simply follow what makes you feel authentic.

How To Be Popular As An Introvert

When you are an introvert, it doesn't automatically mean that you are shy or insecure. Introversion pertains to one's choice to preserve energy instead of being wild and tiring yourself out.

When you are attending a party and when you arrived, you didn't know anyone, just introduce yourself. Simply say "Hi, My name is _____. I don't know anyone here, so I have to introduce myself." Then a fellow guest would reply, "Hello! Nice to meet you. I'm _____." This is a simple way to break the ice.

While you may meet someone friendly, it is also highly likely that you might meet someone unwelcoming. You don't have to worry about them. Just move on and try to mingle with the other guests.

If you meet someone who is nice and confident, they will be more eager to talk to you. It could be the start of a good friendship or even a business partnership.

The more you practice random introduction, the more you can be popular despite the fact that you are introverted.

Abraham Lincoln - The Introverted Orator

The office of the President of the United States is considered the most powerful position in the free world. Many of us think that individuals who have natural charm and social skills are fit to occupy the White House.

However, many great US presidents were introverted such as Abraham Lincoln. A country-laborer turned self-educated lawyer, Lincoln spent most of his nights reading books, which is one characteristic of introverts.

But despite his introversion, Lincoln realized that he can do more by opposing the injustices during his time. Even without powerful allies, massive wealth, or formal education, the political success of Lincoln seems unlikely. While he is silent most of the time, he was authentic when he needed to press on important matters of the state.

While his political opponents were boisterous and gregarious, he was quiet yet confident and always listening. And when he spoke, it was clear that he was carefully listening.

Lincoln sounded authentic because he had genuine empathy towards his fellow man. Matched with vocal power and knowledge drawn from devouring his books, he was noted as a great communicator.

Whether at public speeches or in private meetings, Lincoln was significantly persuasive by imbuing his every word with the depth that it should be shared and not in the way of a fast-talking extrovert.

Chapter Conclusion

The first chapter of this book is critical because it establishes authenticity as the overarching theme that is connected with other ways to become more charismatic.

Remember, the real "you" is the best "you", and the "authentic" way is to be what feels genuine for you whether that's being the life of the party or engaging in deep conversations with smaller groups.

People are naturally drawn towards authenticity, and the relationships that you really care about are the ones that will establish the strongest network that you can build.

Be sure that you understand your options and adjust your behavior to reflect your genuine self. When there are things that you really dread doing, try to reframe your mind so you will better understand the significance of accomplishing that task.

The key to being authentic is the ability to look for something in the situation that will allow you to feel genuine and more acceptable.

Chapter 2 - Build Your Self-Image

In order to establish deeper connections in a more genuine way, you should present the best parts of your authentic self. To put this simply, before you expect others to be attracted to you, you have first to be attracted to yourself.

Chances are, you are already aware of your basic strengths and you can easily exude confidence in different circumstances. However, even the most self-assured person may experience moments of self-doubt. The key is understanding how you can work through them.

Linda is a top sales executive who have experienced moments of self-doubt over the years. She recounted how, as he started garnering recognitions in the company that he would often feel that she just got lucky. Every time, she took these moments of self-doubt as a way to re-evaluate his worth and fortify her self-image by reconnecting with what she knew she could contribute to her workplace.

Over time, she trained himself to embody this awareness. Through a positive self-image, she managed to thrive in her sales career. Many of us are much harder on ourselves than we are on other people.

Is it okay to be judgmental, petty, or mean towards other people? Then, why do you find it okay when you are judgmental, petty, or mean to yourself?
Remember, perception is a reality, and self-image is heavily drawn to self-perception.

When you don't follow up with potential clients, because you assume that they will not buy your product, or when you don't pursue a job application because you assume that you are not qualified, you are only affirming your negative assumptions as your reality.

Whenever you are sabotaging yourself with negative thoughts, you have to ask yourself, "Do I really want this client not to buy from me?" If your response is "No" then you have to change your reality.

The Significance of Self-Image

It can be difficult to make other people believe in your value if you don't even believe in yourself. A negative self-image can significantly affect your decisions, productivity, and personal growth. So why do people hold onto negative self-image?

More often than not, we can gain something when we indulge in negative self-perception. This could be part of our natural instinct to avoid repeating previous mistakes or protecting ourselves against failure. Sometimes, this is also drawn from the desire not to threaten the people around us by challenging the status quo.

Holding yourself back may keep you safe. However, it also means sacrificing how much you can grow and short-changing yourself. Building a positive self-image doesn't necessarily mean that you have to obliterate all doubts and be perfect.

Self-confidence comes from managing your self-doubt and accepting the reality that you are doing something about your flaws, even while understanding these flaws as characteristics that make you likable.

Have you ever had a chance to witness a fashion show? Some outfits are classy, but some are outrageous and out of this world. What are these people thinking? Can you really wear that geometric hat in the workplace? But if you look at the face of the runway models, the attires seemed totally fetching.

Models walk confidently because they know they look good, and they really do. They are completely comfortable, and they show the world that they are likable. As a result, many people admire them. Whatever you think about yourself is who you are.

Activity: Find the Words to Describe Yourself

This activity is designed to help you find the best words that you can use to define yourself. The words that you can identify will compose the description of your strengths that are not only true but the one you can remember when you are having self-sabotaging thoughts.

Free Write

• Grab a piece of paper and a pen and for at least 10 minutes, write down all the positive adjectives that you can use to describe yourself. Then think about how you embody or present the qualities you have written.

• Don't use any filters and don't think too much. Just keep writing. If you are stuck, just rewrite the words that you have already written. Just keep the pen moving.

• Don't just concentrate on the qualities that are important for work. Include all aspects of your life. Do your siblings come to you when they have problems because they know you have the right words to say? Do your friends call you when they are having a difficult time because they know you are a reliable friend? Do your neighbors find you easy to talk with because they feel you are a warm person? Write them all down.

- After 10 minutes, stop writing and read what you have written. Then read again.

Get Feedback

Often, we are blindsided by our own strengths even if they are easily noticed by people around us. So it is crucial to gather information by asking people to describe you.

Make a list of people who really know you well and another list that is composed of your acquaintances.

Then ask these people the following questions (you may also come up with your own set of questions if you want to):

- What's the best word or adjective to describe me?
- What do you think are my best strengths and qualities?

If you are a bit hesitant to ask open-ended questions, you can try presenting characteristics for the person to confirm or deny. Be sure to clarify if you are not clear about or you are surprised by any of the feedback. Why do you think that a particular person chose that word to describe you?

Can that person provide an example of what happened in the past when you have displayed or embodied that characteristic? Make certain that you understand the basis of this comment.

Consolidate

Take a look at what you wrote about yourself and compare it to the feedback you have collected from others.

Select the words that really resonate with you. The words that you choose are genuine for you.

Why Are You So Mean to Yourself?

How do you treat yourself? To figure this out, track it for a week and markdown every self-sabotaging thoughts you have. How often do you give yourself a pat on the back when you did really great?

For every scenario, reward yourself a point. In a week, how many times are you mean to yourself? For each scenario, deduct a point. When a thought began as a negative buy you were able to transform that thought into something positive, reward yourself two points.

Tally your points at the end of each week. Where did you end up? Can you increase your points next week? Figure out whether or not you are really happy with your thought patterns. If not, try to be more proactive about changing your self-image and embracing your thoughts.

Embrace Your Authentic Self

Robert has always wanted to start his own business. For years, he has already made some plans and came up with ideas. However, the venture never materialized because in his head, he had all sorts of reasons why his business would fail.

"I don't have any business experience."

"It's just too hard."

"No one will buy your products".

Robert has always been confident about his strengths, but this didn't stop these thoughts from entering his mind. The effect of his negative self-talk? For years, he failed to take any action at all.

If you are also dreaming of achieving something great - starting your own business, publishing a book, finishing a degree - you have to change your self-perception. It involves the process of continuously reminding yourself that how you plan to succeed in your life is completely up to you.

Changing your perspective about yourself involves actionable steps that can help you reprogram your perceptions and your sense of self-ability so that you have the courage to hustle every day and do the dirty work that you know could help you achieve your dreams.

Self-sabotaging thoughts will not instantly dissipate, and they may never disappear from your life.

However, you can successfully take steps so you can manage your negative self-talk and their influence over you. This will free you to accomplish something difficult.

But how can you develop positive images that will help you fight self-sabotaging thoughts? Here are effective techniques that can help you in this process:

Find a Friend Within

What would you do if you have noticed that one of your closest friends is expressing negative self-thoughts?

Chances are, you would immediately comfort your friend and recite all your friend's amazing characteristics so that the negative thoughts will be transformed from self-sabotaging and damaging to productive and helpful.

Now, what would you do if you have noticed that you are also prone to negative self-thoughts? Can you try becoming a friend for yourself?

Imagine that there are two people behind your back. One is a bully that whispers negative thoughts into your ears, and the other is a cheerleader who reminds you of your goals, strengths, and successes.

When your inner bully begins ranting, stop it immediately and turn to your personal cheerleader.

Don't listen if your bully is shouting "You can't do it, you will never close that sale, you will just stammer, and the client will just insult you!"

Instead, turn to your cheerleader who will say encouraging words to you such as "You have real value that you can offer to this client. You are good at what you do, keeps your promises, and deliver outstanding results. Any client would be lucky to partner with you."

The process can get easier over time. As you increase your awareness of your vulnerability to negative self-thoughts, you can easily catch them, switch on your counterattacks, and become more skilled at changing them into powerful and positive self-image.

Paint a Positive Picture About Yourself

A key element in countering negative self-thoughts is learning how you can reframe your image from bad to good. It is completely up to you if you see a glass as half-empty or half-full. Whatever your frame of mind, it is totally up to your choice.

If you are focusing your mind on things that you cannot do and the things you are afraid to face, then your results will be significantly affected. Reframing your thoughts could change your perspective from certain failures to resounding success, which affects the results of your decisions and actions. Try to embrace your possibilities and veer away from potential failures.

In reframing your mindset, you need to work on your internal and external self.

With internal framing, you can visualize what you want and then mentally practice how it will happen. You can coach yourself to positively think about your strengths, skills, or your tasks. Positive thinking could lead to positive results.

With external framing, you can choose to take your internal thoughts and express them verbally by sharing them with others to provide them with weight and validity.

Claire was an associate creative director at an advertising agency. She expressed her intention to be a partner, even though she'd been there for only five years and the regular track for the partnership was 10 years.

Rather than giving in to her internal bully shouting "You will just waste your time. They will not consider you as a partner." Claire placed her strong belief in her skills and achieved her goal.

She was confident, determined, and consistent, and has proven her worth. Even though she lacks in the required years, her achievements helped her to become a partner on her 7th year in the agency.

Celebrate the Small Victories

One of Edward's greatest dreams is to publish a novel. He already had the story in his mind, and he could see the plot. However, the effort required for the caused a massive dosage of inertia to settle in.

He felt that the goal is a lot bigger than him, and he felt overwhelmed. Before he even started writing he wanted to give up.

However, he started breaking down the process into manageable steps, and immediately, he was able to start writing.

Step 1 - Finalize the story plot

Step 2 - Research on the process of publishing a novel

Step 3 - Learn the important elements of the book proposal

Step 4 - Look for a creative editor

Step 5 - Submit manuscripts to different publishing houses

Edward rewarded himself every time he completed a step to mark his enormous relief and sense of accomplishment.

The rewards were not necessarily expensive ones - some were simple as a movie or a pizza - but they helped Edward feel good about achieving his goals and excited to accomplish the next ones.

While working on his novel, Edward's mindset changed from "This is going nowhere!" to "I can do this!"

Progress regardless of how small it is will help you to feel good. It has a significant effect on our thought patterns as well as our productivity and the way we perceive our own image.

"Fake It Until You Make It"

You are probably wondering why this chapter involves a section about "faking" it. After all, the previous chapter talked about being authentic, and the popular mantra of "fake it until you make it" seems encouraging inauthenticity.

The true purpose of this advice is to try on what it may feel and look like to perceive ourselves in new ways or to act differently than we're accustomed to.

This doesn't mean you have to become a fraud to succeed. Rather, you need to go out of your comfort zone so you can grow comfortable with your changing mindset and until the new reality becomes normal for you.

This is another way to proactively reframe your thoughts as well as your motivations, actions, and decisions.

Fortifying your self-perception is a process, which is crucial to help you improve your charisma.

What Are You Wearing?

While clothes may not define your character, they are perceived as a reflection of your inner state. If you feel tired and lazy and you dress in shapeless, baggy clothes for comfort, you present that lazy aura to the world.

To be more energetic, try putting on some color in your wardrobe. You will observe that the energy tends to stay with you the entire day and that people will transcend that energy back to you. It can be difficult to be prepared and alert if your clothes are gloomy.

If you are "dressed to kill", other people will perceive you in this manner, which reflects it back to you and fortify the thoughts you have about yourself. Self-perception is the basis of how you see yourself and how other people see you.

How to Overcome Shyness

Shyness is a natural emotion when we are in a new environment or if we are not comfortable in dealing with a situation (usually a social setting).

However, there are times that shyness can be debilitating that will prevent you from participating in social situations that are crucial for your personal and professional goals. Perhaps, you really want to meet new people or connect with new business contacts, but you are afraid to be criticized or rejected so you avoid social events.

Studies reveal that shyness is sustained through a vicious cycle in which whenever you approach a social setting, you feel excessive fear, and so you avoid the situation that provides you relief. But this usually results in feelings of self-blame and shame.

In order to cope with these feelings, some people turn their negative thoughts into anger and blame, which significantly decreases your likability.

One way to overcome shyness is to plan for an important social situation ahead.

Remember, introversion doesn't mean shyness. The former is associated with your tendency to reserve energy instead of tiring out. On the other hand, shyness is characterized by your strong tendency to overestimate negative criticism.

Shy people tend to become fearful that others will evaluate them in a negative way. More often than not, people who are timid focus on how to avoid committing errors instead of doing things right.

To reduce your anxiety, you need to spend more time thinking about what you can do to become successful.

If you are due to give a presentation, prepare ahead of time and rehearse your slides. This will significantly reduce your shyness knowing that you have studied well to execute the task excellently, but not necessarily perfectly.

Through preparation, you will be more confident because you will be in control.

Shy Beauty: Nicole Kidman

Nicole Kidman is one of the most recognizable faces on Earth today. She is an award-winning actress and without a doubt oozing with charisma.

But despite her success, she admitted about her shyness. She even stuttered as a kid that she, fortunately, got over and hates going to a party by herself.

To overcome her shyness, Nicole had to practice a lot and come out of her comfort zone. Her shyness in-camera still returns from time to time but manages to deal with it by extensively studying her role.

Chapter Conclusion

In this chapter, we have explored the importance of self-image in improving your likability.

Before you can expect others to like you, you first need to like yourself. Remember, perception is the reality. How you perceive yourself becomes a reality about you, so be nice to yourself.

Being nice, especially to yourself is not just a fuzzy concept. Studies have shown that positive self-talk can pave the way for success and authentic productivity.

Therefore, it is crucial to transform negative self-talk into a positive one by regularly reminding yourself of your accomplishments in the past. This will help you reframe your challenges or obstacles by building clarity about your intended results and celebrating your small wins.

Learning how to fake it is a powerful way to become more familiar with new thought patterns and strategies. Keep on "faking it" until you can feel your new reality that is outside your comfort zone.

Chapter 3 - Be Energetic

In any form of social interaction, every person participates in energy transmission that significantly affects the dynamics of social relationships. Becoming more aware of how we feel and act, how the other person feels and acts, and what mixture contributes to our connection is an important tool for improving likability and nurturing meaningful relationships.

More often than not, we are not aware of the energy we emit that affects our communication. As such, we have no idea if the quality of energy we share is working for us or against us.

Recall a situation that went well for you. Can you still remember your mood at that moment as well as how you approach the situation? How can you describe your energy in that scenario? Regardless of how you describe that moment, it will embody the feelings that people around you at that moment were getting from you.

Highly likable people are full of energy, which is derived from your actual mood in a specific moment and your natural personality. You can feel your own energy in the way you stand and in the way you walk or breathe. The people around you can detect this energy signature that is significantly boosted by your choice of words.

Similarly, you can also be affected by other people's energy, which could impact the quality of our interactions. To put it simply, energy is contagious.

Our own energy could energize other people or even cause them to feel down. Your energy can contribute to team productivity or add confusion. Energy can affect the course of communications and paves way for better connections. Your energy during social situations can be picked up by others and affect the result.

Remember, what you give off is what you can get back. Hence, getting your energy to an optimal place before participating in a situation can make all the difference.
It is crucial to tap the energy that can help you in a particular situation. If you understand that energy is something that you create, you can work on controlling your energy rather than having it control you.

It will help you a lot if you know what energy level you should use in a specific situation or when you need to deal with a specific person.

Using the Right Form of Energy
For other people to perceive you as authentic and sincere, you should be true to yourself and use the right form of energy in a given situation.
It doesn't mean that you have to be loudest in the room. The key here is to be sincere even if you need

to face distractions, difficulties, or challenges. This is crucial to effectively connect with people.

Knowing how to transmit the right energy at the right time and in the right place is a critical part of effectively connecting with others. Just don't forget to be authentic.

Before you can understand the right form of energy to use in a given situation, you must first learn how you can be in tune with it. You should know what kind of vibe you are giving off at any moment so you can determine if it is effective or you need to adjust it.

Are you currently having difficulty in dealing with your coworker? Try adjusting your approach and bring more open and positive energy to the relationship.

Do you find it difficult to motivate your team? Try bringing more energy to the team so they can pick up your vibe, become less combative and achieve some really productive work.

Try to evaluate your energy in a situation and if you think you need to improve, try to adjust. If needed, try tapping into past experiences when you have naturally shared positive energy. You can use these memories so you can change your approach to a new situation or person.

Also, take note that you might need to lead by example. Depending on the energy that other people are contributing to the interaction, it may take some time for them to respond to your energy shift. However, by taking action and calibrating your energy levels, you need to make the first step to bring around more positive results.

Calibrating Your Energy
If you are in a situation where you sense that you are not achieving your intended result, you may calibrate your energy so you can be more open to letting out your more positive and authentic self.

Visualize the emotions that you want to manifest and then recall a memory of a particular time when you have felt that way. Try to recall as many details to make the memory as strong as possible.

Remember the feeling when you have accomplished a task on time and on budget. See the look of admiration from your colleagues. Hear the client comment on the effectiveness of your product.

Try to practice this simple technique, and you will find that your body will relax and you feel more naturally confident and your energy calibrates towards a more positive outlook. Remember this energy shift with you into the situation you are facing and this is the energy that you can give.

Detecting Energy Signals of People Around You

To positively affect the energy of a situation, you need to be conscious not only of our energy signals but also the energy signals of other people.

Rate of speech, tone of voice, body language are all indicators of someone's energy signals. A person who is talking fast and heavily sweats gives off a different energy vibe compared to someone who is speaking calmly with arms crossed. However, you should be open to the fact that you may need clarity in interpreting energy signals.

Crossed arms and downcast look may signal that the person is bored or not interested. But it may also indicate that the person is seriously thinking about a subject. So be sure to ask clarificatory questions if you are not sure of the signals.

Just be careful about your tone and timing when making such clarificatory questions and always use neutral language.

You may use helpful questions such as:

- Is everything okay?
- What do you think about this?
- Can you share what's on your mind?
- Do you want to talk about something?

Speaking Habits of Likeable People

Not everyone is good at initiating and sustaining good conversations. Our speaking style plays a huge part in making certain that our conversations are exciting yet still relevant.

Is there one winning speaking style that you can follow to demonstrate charm? Unfortunately, there is none. However, you can use the following speaking habits used by people who are well-liked.

Be Professional

The first thing that you will notice in the way charming people speak is that they are genuinely professional. They will make you comfortable while always maintaining a professional vibe.

Professionalism is a sign of politeness, so the other person will know that you are a respectful person. This is important if you are speaking with a person you just met.

Avoid Interrupting

This is a classic rule to follow if you want the conversation to be likable. Do not allow yourself to talk if the other person is still talking and making a point. This style will keep the conversation easy and effective.

The habit of butting in will make a massive difference in how you will be perceived by your audience.

Tell the Truth

It can derail the conversation if you begin referring to things that are obviously not true. If you want to be likable, you need to tell the truth at all times. This will make it so much easier for you to relax and ride along the with the conversation. It will also impact your reputation if you lied to a person then eventually he found out the truth.

Be Humble

Likable people are humble. It is easy to spot their lack of ego because it stands out so much in the crowd. Someone who is not in the habit of tooting his own horns is a lot more fun to be with than someone who always likes to talk about himself.

Relax

Chatting with a charming person is easy to follow and naturally enjoyable. This makes a significantly huge difference in terms of how the conversation is going to go. You need to ensure that there's no fear or tension within the conversation, which will provide you the avenue to relax and easily contribute to the conversation.

Tonality

Tonality is an important aspect of communication and the right tonality can help you become more charismatic. It will help you appear confident, intelligent and the impression that you really know what you are talking about. This attracts attention and allows you to be highly likable.

There's no right tonality for every person and every situation. Rather, you can follow a framework that you can customize to a particular personality type.

Pitch

Pitch characterizes how high or low your voice is. In order to maximize attention, you can vary your pitch with tonalities depending on the part of your speech. This will also convey excitement or enthusiasm regardless of the topic you are discussing.

If you are trying to make an assertion or a statement, the most effective tonality is to inflect your speech downward. This will convey that you are confident because you say it with conviction instead of seeking approval.

Volume

If the volume of your voice is too low, people may find it hard to hear you, and others may even dominate your speaking voice. This will not help you assert yourself. While a low voice is usually associated with intimacy and calmness, it lacks the ability to energize the person you are speaking with.

On the other hand, if your voice is too high, people may find you arrogant and rude. Although you may demonstrate enthusiasm, you may struggle to build trust, which is key in likability.

Pace

According to the National Center for Voice and Speech, the recommended pace of words is 2.5 words per second or 150 words per minute.

If you go beyond this pace, your speech may sound rushed and it becomes stressful to listen, especially if you appear agitated.

Speaking a bit slowly will mean that your points will be better understood but will really annoy people who want to know your statement. This will bore your audience, which is not beneficial to you at all.

Learn how to find the right pace, so you are not a bore but not too fast that you feel agitated.

Giving a Great Presentation

Thankfully, you can learn how to give a great presentation. With the right guidance and right practice, you can mesmerize your ideas.

Whether you are a creative director pitching your ideas to the client, a start-up founder convincing a potential investor, or a charity organizer asking for donations, you can benefit from the following ideas to help you give a great presentation:

Frame Your Message

Conceptualizing your message and organizing its structure is an important part of preparing your presentation. Humans are hardwired to respond to stories, so it helps a lot if your message is in a story frame.

You also need to make sure that your story is compelling and will give value to your audience. The goal of your presentation is to ensure that your audience will learn something new or see the world differently afterward.

Plan Your Presentation

After ensuring that your message is clear and valuable, the next step is to focus on how will you actually present your ideas. People will usually deliver their presentation in four ways:

1.   Read the presentation slides or the script from a teleprompter
2.   Prepare bullet points that will help you map out what you want to say in each section
3.   Memorize your talk verbatim or word for word
4.   Familiarize yourself with the core message and deliver it from your heart

The fourth one is the ideal way to deliver your presentation as you can engage your audience and you will really present your authentic self.

Be Comfortable with the Stage

For novice presenters, the idea of facing a crowd can be nerve-wracking. However, experts say that many of us have the tendency to overthink this aspect.

Your success or failure as a presenter will depend on how you are able to make your audience listen to you and how you can make them understand your message, not on how nervous you are. In addition, stage presence is something that you can learn with a bit of coaching.

You don't need to move around. Stand still and use hand gestures to make your point or emphasize an important part of your presentation.

Another important aspect of stage presence is making eye contact. Whenever you are giving a presentation, try to find three to four people in the audience and look them in the eyes.

Eye contact is surprisingly powerful, and this will help you drive your point more than any theatrics.

Take note that there's no good way to deliver a presentation. The most memorable presentations offer a fresh and unique perspective on an idea. The most boring ones are those that are too generic.

However, it may be difficult to find openers that are dependent on the person or situation, especially if you are meeting someone for the first time. There are several generic fallback questions you may use in such situations, so you can use them if needed.

At first, the responses of your conversation partner may sound unenergetic, because most of these questions are quite a cliché already. Nevertheless, you can use responses to determine interesting details about the person.

What do you do?

Even though this one is quite overused, it is also proven effective in initiating conversations. This is a generic question that you can ask anyone.

If you are talking to someone who has retired or whose employment status is not known, you can instead ask "What field you are in?"

In asking this question, you must listen and understand the answer. You really need to hear what the person is saying. Try to find out what value you can offer through his responses and always follow up with new questions.

If they are professionals, you may ask how did they choose their field? If they have their own business, ask what was it like to start as an entrepreneur?

As you will see, the possibilities for engaging in a deeper conversation are quite endless.

All you need to do is to follow your curiosity. If someone asks you the same questions, you should take the chance to open up.

What do you think of the weather?

Another generic conversation starter is to ask about the weather. This icebreaker can lead to trivial small talk or it may result in more valuable connections.

The response may lead to a conversation about the comparisons of the weather in the person's hometown or the challenges of working in deep winter.

It may lead to dialogue about favorite vacation spots or what's the ideal weather for a specific business. Begin with a standard question and be ready to pursue further conversations based on the person's responses.

Sustaining Conversations

To sustain an engaged conversation, you have to learn how to politely probe. A probe is a type of question, which digs deeper into the topic. Probing is useful in exploring new materials for conversations.

Regardless of your curiosity and a long list of follow-up questions, there will be instances in conversations that you will suddenly hit a brick wall. If this happens, it is best to follow the lead of the person that you are trying to engage in a conversation.

If you tried to probe a topic and the other person lost enthusiasm, find a new topic until you find a new one that can help in the dialogue flow again. The more energetic replies you can get, the better your chances for sustaining to probe in ways that can harness connection.

There are three types of probing questions: expansion questions, rational questions, and clarifying questions.

Expansion Questions

These questions are also known as elaboration questions because they delve for more information about a specific response. One popular expansion question is "Can you tell me more?"

This question may invite people to elaborate on something that is interesting to them that naturally makes them feel more comfortable.

It will also allow the people you want to engage with to know that you are really interested in knowing what they are discussing. This places them at ease that they are not dominating the conversation.

Expansion questions will provide you more opportunities to listen and learn the genuine interests, needs, and concerns of the other person and how you may be able to help.

Rational Questions

Rational questions are mainly used to understand the reason behind a stated choice or action. But instead of asking "Why?" you should instead use the question "How come?"

Regardless of your intention, "why" is a word that can easily put the other person on the defensive. This makes people feel as if they are placed on the hot seat and should defend their answers.

On the other hand "How come?" poses a more authentic inquiry that reduces the possibility that the question will be received as some kind of attack. You should also try to watch your rate of speech and tone of voice.

Longer probes like "I'm really curious, what made you let go of your job to start your own business?" feels more genuine and less aggressive compared to a generic and lightning-fast "How come?"

Clarifying Questions

Clarifying questions will show that you are paying attention to the person you are talking with. Summarize or rephrase what you have heard and ask if you really got it, or if you don't think that you have understood, be sure to ask the person to provide more details.

Clarifying questions are also great conversation stallers because they will buy you time if you are thinking about where you want to take the conversation next. But be careful how you phrase your clarifying questions.

Stay away from openers like "Are you saying...?" that, depending on your tone and whom you are talking to, can be wrongly received as outrage, judgment, or shock.

Rather, you can paraphrase what you think you heard and then check if you really got it right.

Never Interrogate

When you are probing, be sure not to interrogate the person. Never ask any questions unless you really want to know the answer. Chances are, you will just tune out if the other person replies and you really don't care.

If you ask something that genuinely interests you, the follow-up questions will come naturally and your body language, as well as energy, will reflect your interests. Just be careful not to let your enthusiasm tip over into a rapid-fire.

Firing people with machine-gun questions, regardless of your exuberance, may make them feel as if they have to defend themselves, so they will do so.

Take note that conversations are two-sided, filled with breaks and spontaneous chats during which the people talking with each other consider and absorb what is being discussed.

Opening up and sharing information about yourself is also critical because it helps in building a bond that good communication can harness. This makes you more charismatic and makes people around you comfortable enough to share.

Chapter Conclusion

In this chapter, we have explored the importance of curiosity in harnessing our charisma. This can be done by engaging in meaningful conversations that can be sustained by asking the right questions.

In conversations, we appear more comfortable and authentic if you remain curious. You can do this even without deeper knowledge of the person you are speaking with.

Curiosity will bring out the best in you and will prompt you to naturally do all the things that can foster positive connections.

Chapter 4 - Cherish Similarities and Honor Differences

Learning that we share a connection with a person can help us to be more comfortable, regardless of the connection is trivial or a more serious one. The similarities might be having mutual friends, liking the same food, or have had similar experiences.

Realizing those genuine similarities as well as associations could increase your ease with new people, and also, their comfort with you. Being comfortable not only makes communication easier but can also open new windows to discover new things. This is key to building more meaningful connections.

At first, the similarities we have with people may not be obvious. However, learning how to stay alert to these commonalities is part of the work of establishing connections into deeper relationships.

As we pursue our careers, we often cease finding similarities with people we know. We may think we have already learned all the information we need about them.

Taking a closer look at our existing relationships is another helpful approach to continue nurturing our relationships. This includes relearning our curiosity about the people we know and staying conscious of the things we may share aside from the task at hand.

The Importance of Likability

Our level of comfort increases when we meet someone with whom we have strong commonalities. Our charm becomes effective as the conversation flows naturally.

In general, people tend to like people who are like them. Of course, this doesn't mean that you can magically sense this whenever you meet someone. There are just instances that the commonalities are too strong, and you may also come up against the same characteristics that you may not like.

In such instances, it is ideal that you step back if you can and evaluate your resistance. There are also instances that the commonalities are direct and explicit, and sometimes they are more subtle that can only be detected over time.

But once we discover our commonalities, we can build opportunities for more meaningful and more genuine relationships. The path towards likability can become shorter and smoother. As the comfort level increases, communication becomes more open that builds more trust.

While you can't automatically achieve likability, you can easily start building it by finding similarities.

Trust and Likability

We usually trust other people in our line of work to recommend a vendor or a product. We often shortlist a candidate for a job because a trusted colleague had a positive experience in working with that person in the past.

Trust is a key element in likability because people trust the sources they really know best. This is the same principle behind your willingness to go on a blind date arranged by someone you really know. In your mind, "Roger knows her, and Roger knows me, so I can trust that at the least, she's a decent, normal lady."

This is also the reason why many companies are fond of offering referral programs. If a company already has employees whom they genuinely trust, then it is easy to tap this resource in looking for new staff members.

Validating our choices is important for harnessing likability. We connect to a person or a brand through a third party that we trust. We ask our neighbors for the number of a good gardener. We ask colleagues with similar tasks for tool recommendations. We trust parents with kids the same age as ours for advice about pediatricians and tutors. If our friend trusts a particular person, we find it easy to like that person, too.

Discovering Similarities

There are numerous ways we can be associated or similar to another person. This point can be easily illustrated through social media sites such as Facebook. How many degrees of separation are you away from people you don't know? Try to use Facebook to search for people you share the same name who are living in your suburb.

Chances are, you will see several people who have the same first name as you who are living nearby, and some of them know people who are in your list of friends.

Similarities are all around us, even if they are not obvious at first. Having mutual friends is just one way to increase your likability. We may learn other areas of commonality as well like common experience, work histories, shared educational backgrounds, demographic similarities, and shared values and beliefs. All these are possible ways to create the basis for genuine connection.

When we first meet someone, we often ask generic questions such as:
- Where do you work?
- Where did you grow up?
- Where did you go to school?

Learning information that matches our own can easily increase our interest and excitement in the new person. Finding the similarity could easily lead to sustained conversation and will result in deeper connection.

Commonalities that may not be obvious at first can come to the surface easily with the right types of questions. Avoid interrogating someone by rapid-fire questions. Be sure that you also share important aspects of yourself.

Self-disclosure is crucial if commonalities are going to be effectively discovered. You may mention your organizational affiliations, places you have lived, your interests or hobbies.

You can also allow the other person to discover similarities by learning about their backgrounds and interests as well as finding common territories. With this, you can further harness your capacity to build stronger relationships. The more information you know about the person, the stronger the foundation you can build on.

Shared Passion

Shared passion can bring people together in ways that are stronger compared to other relationships. If we are passionate about a specific interest, the experience is emotionally powerful. The connection can be intense and fast if you share the same feelings with a person.

If you are a dog parent and you see someone who loves his canine friend, you can easily feel the same passion as that person. There are times that these shared beliefs are quite apparent because of the context in which you meet - at a park walking your pets, at a house of worship, or an industry conference.

In some instances, you may need to ask questions to determine if you have shared passion. Below are some questions that you can ask to figure out if there are potential connections you can find through shared passion:

- I am interested in sharing my time and talent as a volunteer in a local organization. Can you recommend a local charity or civic group?
- We just moved to the neighborhood. Can you recommend a place to unwind?
- What do you think about the current city mayor?
- Are you happy with our congressman's recent actions?
- Can you recommend a local church or temple?

Religion and politics are two subjects that many people feel passionate about. So these are interesting areas that you can explore. Just be sensitive about intense emotions and try to consider changing the topic or backing off if the conversations become too heated.

Remember, your goal is to establish a connection and not find an enemy.

The Art of Mirroring

Some commonalities are easy to see such as an action or a way of speaking. When we feel at ease in a situation, we mirror back those things when we communicate in some way.

This is usually done unconsciously but a distinct way we can relate when they feel connected.

Mirroring usually happens without thinking. However, it can also be used in conscious methods to provide more comfort to a situation or express understanding. If a person is telling you something excitedly, leaning forward in his chair, it may also help communicate your interest if you use body language that mirrors this behavior. So, you may also lean forward.

On the other hand, leaning away could indicate detachment, which is the exact opposite of what we are after. Leaning forward builds a similarity that could lead to better understanding.

It will feel natural even if you are aware that you are mirroring someone else's action. However, forcing it will be too obvious. Don't overdo it. Just be aware how you are genuinely experiencing the conversation and allow your movements to mirror the engagement.

Similarities Could Help Set the Mood

If you want to be more likeable, it is ideal to look for similarities when you are meeting new people. It will help you to build trust, wherever and whatever those commonalities might be. As we pursue our careers, we may experience narrowing down our repertoire for dealing with new situations. So, it is crucial to keep harnessing our social skills.

Ask questions so you can be attuned to the wide range of information you receive in response. There are a lot of ways that you may connect with someone, and through genuine curiosity and listening skills, you may discover what you have in common with someone and where your genuine connections happen.

Similarities build the foundations for trust if you are forging new relationships. Just as it is essential to figure out similarities to help in establishing genuine comfort in personal relationships, it is important to end a conversation with those feelings of trust.

How to Be Charming Without Trying

There are people who seem naturally charming. Whatever they do (even if they are not doing anything) they are perceived to be as charming.

People are naturally drawn to them, and they are very fun to be with.

It can be hard to fake your behavior so more people will like you. In order to be charming without trying, you should be authentic.

Remember, being genuine makes you likeable. Be genuinely curious about people, and if you are really curious, make certain that you are polite.

Unfortunately, there are people who are curious but could be intrusive. Yes, you may ask questions, but never interrogate the person as if you are trying to extract the truth.

Another simple way to be charming without too much effort is to smile. This easy gesture can make you appear more attractive instantly.

Happiness is an attractive feature in both men and women who are highly charismatic. Those who are naturally happy and always smiling are like magnets that attract people. So smile so you can feel better about everything in your life.

Chapter Conclusion

In this chapter, we have explored the importance of finding similarities to increase our likability. Remember, people like people who are like them.

In the same vein, people trust people they know best. Being affiliated with a trusted source will usually mean that this element of trust can be transferred to you.

Discovering similarities is also key to improve our charisma. Try to determine common backgrounds and interests, shared experiences and beliefs to look for similarities that could help you in building connections with other people.

The subtle art of mirroring can also help you harness your likability. If you are comfortable in a conversation and you feel engaged, you can communicate this by reflecting it through your body language.

Chapter 5 - Give Value

One of the best ways to become charismatic and build a connection is to show that we understand the needs of other people, and we are happy to fulfill them.

By using the lessons you have learned in the previous chapters, you can be creative to expand the types of value we can offer to other people.

In most instances, people are willing to share, because they are expecting something in return. However, you can provide genuine value if you learn how to give simply because you want to.

Sharing creates value, which doesn't always mean making grand gestures or exerting major effort.

Even in your own little ways, you can send a clear signal that you are thinking about the other person and that you are genuinely interested to help.

More often than not, it is easy to see how you can help a person. Sometimes, it is not obvious, especially if the person is far more superior than you.

However, everyone needs and appreciates a helping hand. Regardless of your status in life, you can always bring value to someone else.

Providing assistance is one of the best ways to increase your charisma as it opens the door to building the relationship.

With each interaction, you can increase your similarity and familiarity.

How to Provide Value to Another Person

There are endless ways to bring value to another person, and anyone has something to offer.

Whether it's by offering feedback and support, building opportunities for meaningful interactions, or sharing resources, you can always share by finding more opportunities to give back.

People have the tendency to react to situations in the same manner that works on a particular level. If something has worked out in the past, there's a big chance that it will be effective again in the future. However, sticking only to the proven methods can narrow down our perspective of what we are capable of doing for other people.

Probably, we feel as if we don't have the time and the resources to share. Sometimes, we are not sure if giving will be appropriate.

By widening our perspectives and broadening our creativity in handling situations, we can understand that sharing is a continuous process and can benefit you throughout your career.

In seeking opportunities to help other people, you can identify all the ways that can bring value to your relationships.

Personal and Business Connections

One way to bring value to another person is to be a matchmaker. When you meet someone, try thinking about other people whom they might be interested to meet.

When you become a matchmaker, you can leverage all other lessons you have learned in this book.

You can be curious about the person, and then your interest will be awakened if you identify commonalities.

Before you introduce people, you should always ask them if they want to be introduced, because you should only connect people if they are both interested.

You should also be mindful that introductions can also affect the reputation of a person, so it is best to be careful about this.

By establishing connections between two people for whatever reason, you can create meaningful interactions that will further increase your likability.

How To Be The "Cool One"
Contrary to the common belief, being "cool" is not about you, but it is about other people.

This involves their expectations and perceptions. Here are a few things you should know if you want to be perceived as a cool person.

Wear Proper Clothes

If you are not conscious about how you wear your clothes, other people may take you for a slob who doesn't take yourself seriously.

Just think about the cool people you know, and how they dress properly to set the expectation.

Some guy with messy hair walks into a conference wearing a black shirt, a pair of rugged blue jeans, and wearing a dirty pair of sneakers. What do you think about this guy?

Probably like "Man, this person is an outsider".

You might be an interesting person, but very few people will actually give you their attention just because you failed to live up to the expectation of a cool person.

So does this mean we need to wear a tuxedo? Now, that's ridiculous. Formal wear has their purpose, but so do jeans and shirts.

If you want to be the coolest guy in the room, you need to wear clothes that are suitable for the environment.

Be Interesting

Cool people are really interesting. Certainly, it may be difficult to tell if you're really interesting or if the other person is just really polite. However, it is quite easy to tell the difference.

If the other person finds you interesting, they will ask questions to look for more information. If they are just nodding, then you can't say that they are really into you.

Moreover, if they move closer to you, then there's a good chance that the person finds you interesting. Of course, this could be because they want to hear you better, but psychologists reveal that this is actually a subconscious signal that they really find you interesting.

Use the Appropriate Body Language

As you will later learn in the next chapter, nonverbal communication such as body language can be used to become more likeable.

If you want to convey that you are a cool person, do not cross your arms as this indicates that you are closed off and you are not willing to engage in any conversation.

For you to become the coolest guy in the room, you should learn how to use your body language to your benefit.

How can you achieve this? You can smile, laugh, and use kind gestures. Use the right tonality of your voice that is proper for your environment. Convey your charm through your posture and movements.

Being the coolest person in the room is not something that you can master in a few days, but it can be achieved.

With the tips discussed above, and regular practice, you can really enhance your charisma to help you achieve your business and personal goals.

Chapter Conclusion

Learning how you can provide value to the people you engage with is key in improving your likability. Learn how to give, because you can and because this act brings value to the relationship that you are trying to establish.

There are many ways that you can bring value to other people such as playing matchmaker to people who may mutually benefit from each other, giving advice, doing favors, sharing resources, and extending invitations to interesting activities and events.

Try to be proactive in determining how you could help the people in your social circle. You can do this by making an action plan that details what you need to do, who you will do it for, and when you want to make that plan happen.

Always remember in the law of karma - what comes around, goes around. You will reap rewards in return, if you have the habit of giving.

You will significantly increase your chances to be a likeable person if you know how to pay it forward. You can repay the generosity you have received by continuing the chain.

Chapter 6 - Be Memorable

Who is your closest friend? Try to visualize the last time you spent time with this friend. How does this particular memory make you feel? Do you feel great about just thinking about it?

Now, think about a conversation you had recently that didn't go so well. Maybe you were cornered at the office by an annoying colleague or you got trapped in a conversation with someone who was really creepy at a bar. Think about having to meet that person again.

The way you experience a situation or a person - the emotions you feel, whether positive or negative - could still linger in your memory.

Experts call this mood memory, which is the impression or emotion you associate with a person or a particular event. A key part of improving your charisma is creating positive memories of yourself to other people.

Surprisingly, it's not totally what you said that can bring happy memories to a person. Try to think about a person that really makes you feel good. Can you remember a conversation with this person? Probably. But it can be difficult to remember the conversation.

Was it the general outlook on things or the person's mannerisms? Even if you can't figure out the exact reasons why you feel good when you remember that person, you just feel good about it all. People will remember you more on how you made them feel than what you have said.

The person who can naturally tell jokes without being offensive can leave everyone in a more positive mood. However, the person who always dismisses your ideas and often rude can bring negative energy.

Memories are encoded not only as sensory information but also as emotional information. This is why whenever we recall a memory, we usually find ourselves reminiscing the feelings we experienced when it first happened.

The lingering remembrance of feeling (the positive memory) is important of charisma. If people have a positive mood memory of you, they will be happy to hang out with you or do business with you.

Jokes That Make People Instantly Like You (Ellen DeGeneres Style)

Ellen DeGeneres is one of the funniest celebrities today. By learning from her wit and humor, you can learn the proper way to joke around so people will find your likable and not offensive.

By using the right form of humor, you can easily win people over and create the right impression by making them smile or even laugh.

According to experts, Ellen employs three kinds of jokes that disarms her guests and make them like her instantly. Read on and find out if you can also use these jokes to enhance your charisma.

1.   Ego Booster Jokes

Don't you love it when someone compliments you? But instead of direct compliment, you can instead inject some humor.

In one awards night, Ellen was hosting the show and said to Amy Adams who received several nominations for two films:

"...that's so (what's the word for it) selfish."

People will instantly like you if you make them laugh while also highlighting their success.

2.   Poking Fun Jokes

One perfect example of this joke is when Jennifer Lopez was a guest on Ellen's show.

Jennifer shared that she had bronchitis, and then later on when the star touched Ellen, the comedienne reached for a tissue to wipe her hands as if her guest gave her bacteria.

Even though that joke was poking fun of Jennifer's bronchitis, it was totally in good faith as it didn't alienate the guest because there's no harm in the fact that she got sick.

However, you need to be careful in cracking this type of joke. Be sensitive as some people are insecure if you poke fun of things that are core to their identity or if you are making fun of something that is permanent.

For example, don't make fun of people who have abnormal gait as it is really offensive and could be perceived in bad taste.

Self-Deprecating Jokes

Jokes that are meant to ridicule yourself are usually harmless. For example, when Rihanna was a guest at Ellen's show, the host asked her about her birth year. When Ellen learned that it was 1988, Ellen playfully replied, "I still have shoes from '88", which implies that she was already old.

Making fun of yourself is an effective way to make people like you. You may make fun of other people but be careful to only do this to your closest friends. It is usually not okay to make fun of people you just met, especially in a business setting.

Use Your Energy, Body, and Words

In the previous chapters, we have explored how our choices of words, body language and energy could affect not only our perception of ourselves but also the perception of other people on us. These elements are crucial to position your image as a positive one.

The energy that enters a situation could dictate your choices of words as well as body language. These elements transfer your energy to other people that in turn affects their memory about you and the situation. This is a cycle and one that you can easily affect you when you are conscious.

Energy Transfer

Bear in mind that energy is contagious. If you really want to make others feel good, you should also feel good. This doesn't mean that you should always be happy. You just need to connect with what feels positive and proper in the situation as well as the person you need to deal with.

When you are aware of this, you can consciously shift your level of energy to fit a particular situation. Consider what energy will work best for you at that moment, and if needed, try to remember a time when you were energetic.

Concentrate on as many details as you can to remember what it felt like, and try to internalize it. The key is not to fake the mood but instead, find or re-create the mood within yourself.

Body Language

According to Albert Mehrabian, a renowned psychologist, body language contributes more than 50% to our charisma.

If you want your genuine image to linger with someone after the conversation, you must make certain that what you say during the interaction is true with how you say it.

Your verbal, as well as non-verbal messages, should communicate with the same things. There are many subtleties in body language.

It is often challenging to learn the rules for non-verbal communication because of the variables in style, gender, and cultural differences. However, there are some general ways you can communicate through your gestures that are important to focus on.

Be mindful of the following aspects of body language if you wish to increase the potential for building positive memories:

Smiling

There's power in a genuine smile. It can convey openness, trustworthiness, and approachability. Perhaps, this is the single most immediate way to communicate likability. A genuine smile can build strong positive mood memories. People can remember your smile even if they cannot remember what you've said.

You can use your smile as an invitation to engage a conversation and feel comfortable saying what is really in your mind. Not all of us can naturally smile, but this can be achieved through practice. Gradually, muscle memory will take over and it will be easier for you to naturally smile.

Eye Contact

Consistent eye contact can make a person feel respected and listened to. There is numerous research that provides veracity to this claim. Direct eye contact can release feel-good endorphins and the heart begins to beat a bit faster.

Of course, this doesn't mean that you should be staring at someone relentlessly. The goal is to be charismatic and not to be creepy. Just follow your natural instincts to sustain eye contact to show that you are listening and understanding what the other person is saying.

Nodding

Nodding is another powerful non-verbal signal, albeit can be specific to gender. Body language experts suggest that women nod to show that they are listening, while men nod if they agree with something.

Regardless if you are a man or a woman, you should be conscious of how much you are doing it. Remember, nodding should be a non-verbal cue.

Overdoing this non-verbal signal will defeat its purpose. In the same vein, paying attention to when you must nod may actually help you convey how much you are experiencing the situation.

Nodding can effectively convey that you understand what you are hearing especially if backed up by quick verbal signals such as "I agree with you" or "That's really interesting".

Personal Space

Personal space refers to the physical distance between two people when they are in a conversation. There are two primary things that can affect how a person feels about personal space: communication style and culture.

In some cultures, such as in India, they are comfortable with intimacy. It is okay with friends to hold each other even if they are just casually talking. On the other hand, some cultures in Northern Europe such as in Finland, people prefer to maintain more distance.

If you go to India, you will commonly see groups of male friends walking together with arms draped around each other or even holding hands. If you travel to Finland, you will see people standing a bit apart.

Word Choice

Bear in mind that the words we use—in thinking or in speaking— are our choice that reflects the way we think. Using positive frames can help you stick to your genuine thoughts while providing you the opportunity to express them in a positive light.

Be conscious of your word choice, and always make sure to be positive.

"I don't have the easiest job."

This sentence alone is a good example of positive word choice.

"I have a difficult job."

Now, that sentence is basically synonymous with the first one. However, there's a significant difference between the two methods of framing the essential fact.

By choosing to say you don't have the easiest job, you can make it easy for the next thought to be "But it isn't the most difficult job, either."

Choosing this method can immediately direct your thinking to the positive and balances of energy that are more neutral.

Aside from word choice, you also need to express your thoughts. This is an effective way to manage internal distractions and increase your listening capacity.

The key is to not allow people to misinterpret what's going on in your mind if you can just tell them.

Ask For Advice

Conveying your authentic interest in someone by following your natural curiosity could help in building connections and open more opportunities to improve relationships.

To be more memorable, talk to the people you really admire and ask for advice. When you ask someone for their expertise or advice, you are sending a message that you value that person.

This builds a positive memory because people basically feel recognized and respected for their strengths when other people are seeking advice from them. Similarly, you are leveraging your curiosity and building opportunities to learn. Seeking out advice could leave you vulnerable, but eventually, you can use this for your own benefit.

Being vulnerable is being open and genuine, which are charming traits. By having the confidence to expose yourself, you can open up the door for sustained communication. In business settings, mentor-mentee dynamics is a classic advice-seeking relationship.

This connection could be effectively developed with someone you already know. But you can also try to set this connection with people you just met for the first time.

As a mentee, you may feel that you are taking more value than what you can offer. This is okay as eventually, you will have your chance to provide value to your mentor.

Also, bear in mind that people really like to be recognized and valued for their expertise. By asking for advice, you can create a positive mood memory that helps in sustaining relationships so that it will continue to evolve.

How to End a Conversation

It is not always easy to know when to end a conversation. Ending it too soon may convey the message that you are not interested, or you would rather be talking to someone else or do something else.

On the other hand, talking out too long may create the impression that you don't respect the time of the other person or you are not sensitive to the subtle signals that the other person wants to go out of the conversation.

Try to leave the conversation with the other person yearning a bit more of you and feeling energized from the interaction. If you have the power to read people's minds as you ending the conversation, ideally, you will think something like this:

- "It was nice to talk to you; I hope to meet you again, soon."
- "I'm ecstatic that you asked for my advice. It gave me an opportunity to help, and it made me feel valued and recognized."

If you are not sure if you want to end the conversation, you can try the following subtle tactics, which can provide the other person a chance to stop the conversation or continue if they want to.

- "Can I grab you a drink?" - This conversation curtailer can create an easy way to the exit. You may say "I'm getting myself a drink; do you want one?". This will allow for both possibilities - continuation or exit. Learn how to take a cue from the response of the person.

- "Should we mingle? This one is applicable to almost any situation. Joining a crowd with someone else can create opportunities to re-energize the conversation or open up new subjects to discuss.

- "I need to go there." This approach is quite useful in a workshop or conference setting. You can try saying "I want to go check out that booth, do you like to join me?" It conveys that you are not trying to get rid of the person because you are even open to the possibility of exploring more of the conference with him.

Before ending the conversation, try to make the other person feel good and try to ask for another chance to reconnect. Ending the conversation with a good impression will leave the door open so you can follow up with the person. Many conversations naturally end, with or without the help of any conversation ender.

In such cases, if it is clear that it is time to end the conversation, you can pair your words with body language. This includes picking up your bad, looking at your watch, putting on your coat, or extending your arm for a handshake.

Basically, being memorable is all about creating a positive impression. There are numerous ways to be memorable, but the most effective one is always show your authentic self.

Chapter Conclusion

In this chapter, we have explored the importance of leaving a positive impression to enhance your charisma.

Always remember that people are more willing to remember how you made them feel compared to what you said.

The energy you share usually has more of a lasting impression on someone compared to the exact words you have said.

In improving your charisma, you can use effective word choices, body language, and energy shifts. How you perceive and present yourself can significantly affect the impression you leave.

Conclusion

Charisma is more than a cheeky idea or a concept of which you must stay conscious - it is an outlook to your life and the people around you.

The point of harnessing your likability is not for you to be agreeable to everyone and for everyone to be agreeable with you. Rather, the point is to build valuable connections that could help your productivity, your social health, your relationships, and the quality of your life.

Be genuine in your interactions and follow what you really want to do and not what you think you must do. Even though the overarching principle was discussed in Chapter 1 - Be Authentic - this book is not intended for linear understanding. All the methods described in this guide are intertwined and can work in harmony with one another.

Based on how you want your relationships to succeed and where you are in your career, you can focus on each method that will be most valuable for you at present.

Select one and work on integrating this into your interactions with the people around you. Eventually, that approach will be second nature to you, and so you can move on to the next approach to focus on.

If you enjoyed this book, please take the time to leave me a review where you purchased this book from.

I appreciate your honest feedback, and it really helps me to continue producing high-quality books.

Best wishes

Darcy Carter

Reading People:

Harness the Power Of Personality, Body Language, Influence and Persuasion To Transform Your Work, Relationships & Boost Your Confidence!

Contents

__Introduction__

Imagine a life where you can easily read people. Where you can tell if someone is having a negative or a positive effect on you. Or if they really like you or not? Imagine the value your life would receive if you could discover when someone was lying to you. Or if they really had your best interests in mind.

Think about how such an ability could help you excel in life. Imagine if after meeting someone you could gain real insights into their true personality to find out what type of person they really are. In fact you could even use this knowledge to take a look at your own personality to see what it might reveal about you.

Reading people is a powerful way to realize people's intentions, figure out who is sincere, manage relationships and much more. The ability to quickly read a person gives us a massive advantage in business, love and life. These abilities might seem like they're straight out of a superhero movie. But the truth is that with the right knowledge you can get a glimpse into a person's mind and know what they're really thinking.

Every second of every day, everybody around you is broadcasting a signal. Your ability to read other people depends on how well you're able to read those signals. It is a skill that you can use to improve every area of your life. With enough practice reading people quickly and effectively will become more natural for you.

The first thing you need to do in learning how to read people is to become more self aware. That is, you have to be aware of when you form opinions about other people. At a certain point, between meeting a stranger, and then interacting with them you will start to form an opinion of them. That could be, "I just don't trust this person". Or "This person is really cool" and so on. The truth is, only a few minutes have passed. You aren't aware of their history and don't know much about them. Whatever they say could be real, lies, or otherwise. Intuition is what you are tuning into. When you get good at noticing how you feel about people you become better at picking up on clues and reading people.

Reading people involves listening, observing and then understanding. Every person gives away clues all the time and everyone has individual personalities. Always be on the lookout for them. During every interaction you should be collecting information and summarizing it. Then you can calibrate your demeanor and communication to suit them and the result will be higher quality interactions.

When you start reading people begin with an open mind. Approach all of your interactions with a blank slate and no judgement. You can start out with small talk to familiarize yourselves. Whilst some people are confident and outgoing there are others who will be more reserved and shy. When you come across shy people they might seem a little antisocial or standoffish. However don't take it personally just go slowly and get them talking. Let them know you are friendly by smiling at them. It doesn't matter if they smile back or not, take the first step. Smiling will send them a positive first message about yourself.

Always make the first move. You can then introduce yourself and have a topic ready to get things rolling. You could bring up a funny story or something situational such as the setting your in or a movie you watched recently and so on. Taking the initiative will take the pressure off them. At the outset you should speak for eighty percent of the time. Avoid asking too many questions early on and try just to keep talking.

When it comes to asking questions go with open ended questions. You want to elicit the most informational responses that keep conversations going. Closed ended questions that elicit yes or no responses will stop the conversation. Focus on questions with, how, what, when, why, or who in them. At the start conversations light and cordial. If you want to go deeper then you can try revealing weaknesses of yours. This will make people more comfortable with you and more likely to open up information to you.

Listen actively, this means really tuning into what people are saying and showing interest in it. Shy people will be more sensitive so show some empathy to them. Repeat what they and try to summarize the points, then follow up with deeper questioning. Avoid interrupting or dominating the chat. Try to resist any of that. If there is silence be comfortable with that and give them the opportunity to fill it. Sometimes shy people will be hesitant to speak and you may need to give them more time.

Monitor how engaged they are. Tell tale signs are their level of eye contact and how much they speak. If they don't show much eye contact or only reply with short answers then you need to work on better engagement with them. Stick with the subjects they like and drill deeper into those subjects with more open ended conversations.

If they really aren't interested just smile and move on. Always be gracious and polite. On the other hand if you had a good conversation you can invite the person out again. From there you can develop a relationship. Exchange contact information and set ip something low pressure such as after work drinks. Or if your conversations were on activities and hobbies you could lead that into going to do those things.

Remember that when you are reading people try to be subtle about it. Many people might become defensive if you are being over analytical of them. Ideally you should observe others without them knowing about it which will produce the most accurate readings.

How you spend your time will affect your ability to read people. If you spend long periods of time alone or working on computers then it's going to be more difficult to read people. That also includes excessive use of smart phones, tablets and so on.

To begin reading people we must understand personality.

Part One: Personality

Have you ever wondered why people behave a certain way or why they react in different ways? Have you ever wished to understand someone better? Or how to get along with people at work?

The way we react and behave is different from others because we all have our own desires, fears and individual personalities. We are motivated by our thoughts and our actions are the result.

When you understand yourself and the people around you it will improve your professional and personal relationships. Knowing a person's personality type will improve your interactions. In addition this will remove any pre judgements or first impressions.

In the following chapters we will explore various personality measuring tools and types to help you read people.

The Big Five Personality Traits

Personality is a massive influence on the way that a person reacts to various situations. Psychologists have identified five traits of personality that describe the character of a person. These personality traits influence behaviour, relationships, career path, lifestyle and more. They are a key indicator in reading people.

Each person will have their own characteristic personality traits that will prevail throughout their life. Typically one trait will be more dominant in certain people. The dynamics of someone's family, their relationships and upbring will also affect these traits. Research points towards nurture being accountable to half of the influence whilst the other half depends on their environments. From childhood to adulthood personality tends to remain relatively stable.

The big five traits of personality are, extroversion, openness, conscientiousness, neuroticism and agreeableness. When you are interacting with people look out for these characteristics.

Let's take a look at them in more depth.

Openness

High Score	Low Score
• Enjoy trying new things	• Dislikes change
• Creative	• Traditional thinking
• Enjoy challenges	• Not very imaginative
• Good imagination	• Dislikes theoretical concepts

People with high levels of openness are more open minded and receptive to new ideas. They are adventurous, like to be challenged and enjoy experiencing new things. High scorers in openness are creative and inquisitive to learn new things that enhance their knowledge. Low scorers tend to be more conservative. They dislike anything foreign or unfamiliar but are quite efficient. However a mixture of high and low levels of openness can be useful depending on the situation. People high in openness tend to do well in creative pursuits such as science and the arts. Those having lower levels of openness tend to work well in accounting, law and sales.

Conscientiousness

High Score	Low Score
• Orderly	• Less organized
• Goal driven	• Procrastinates
• Pays attention to detail	• Impulsive
• Persistent	• Messy

Discipline and dutifulness are two important aspects of the conscientiousness personality. High scorers are well organized, hard-working, self disciplined and efficient. They are goal driven, perfectionists who tend to be workaholics. This manifest in their life, for instance with clean and well organized homes. On the other hand people low in conscientiousness can be seen as more spontaneous and playful. They find it hard to motivate themselves and are often unorganized.

People high in conscientiousness tend to do well in jobs that allow for planning and goal setting such as executive roles or sales. Whilst those having lower levels of conscientiousness tend to work well in less structured roles such as freelancing or independent business.

Extraversion

High Score	Low Score
• Make friends easily	• Worn out after socializing
• Energized by other people	• Dislikes small talk
• Says things before thinking	• Prefers solitude
• Seeks excitement or adventure	• Difficult to start conversations

High scorers in extraversion are outgoing, assertive, cheerful and enjoy social interactions. This has a significant impact on social behavior which results in strong social skills and an active social calendar. On the other hand they are extremely uncomfortable spending time alone. Low scorers in extraversion are more reserved, quiet and prefer more time alone. That does not necessarily mean they are antisocial but typically require less stimulation and may become easily worn out in social activities.

People high in extraversion tend to do well in roles that involve engaging with people such as teaching, politics and sales. Whilst those having lower levels of extraversion tend to work well in less public roles such as writing or the arts.

Agreeableness

High Score	Low Score
• Always ready to help	• Stubborn
• Feels empathy for others	• Insults and belittles others
• Interested in others	• Manipulative
• Caring and honest	• Self-centered

High scorers in agreeableness are kind, altruistic and tolerant. Getting along with others is important to them and thus they are flexible and reluctant to criticize or judge people. Politeness and compassion are the hallmarks of people with this personality trait. They are good hearted people who are extremely cooperative, empathetic and trustworthy. However, agreeableness is not useful in situations requiring tough or objective decisions.

People low in agreeableness tend to be skeptical, argumentative, selfish and blunt. They also are defensive of their beliefs and can sometimes be overly judgemental of others.

People high in agreeableness tend to make great leaders in companies, politics and education. Whilst those having lower levels of agreeableness do well in workplaces where they need to make hard decisions and deliver bad news such as managerial roles.

Neuroticism

High Score	Low Score
• Stressed easily	• Calm in stressful situations
• Worries about many things	• Optimistic
• Easily upset	• Emotionally stable
• Mood swings	• Rarely feels sad or depressed

People high in neuroticism are usually emotionally unstable and get upset easily. Often a person who is moody, worries about things and gets irritated or nervous frequently. Managing stress is a challenge for them and they easily succumb to negative moods. Studies conclude that dominance in this personality trait makes a person more susceptible to depression.

On the other side, low scorers in neuroticism are more calm and less likely to worry. Thus being low in neuroticism may be considered to be an advantage. However it can make people too careless and likely to downplay potential threats.

People who are higher in neuroticism tend to work well in safe and secure environments that allow them creative space such as design and writing. Whilst those having lower levels of neuroticism tend to thrive in environments that utilize their composed temperament. Potential job ideas are, law and psychiatry.

Introverts and Extroverts

An easy way to read people is to find out if a person is introverted or extroverted. Once you understand how this works you can improve your interactions with others.

The late 20th-century Swiss psychiatrist Carl Jung popularized the use of introvert and extrovert personality types to help with understanding the various attitudes and behaviors of his patients.

Introverts are people whose attention and focus is usually directed inwards to their thoughts and feelings. Whereas an extrovert's are people whose attention is directed more towards the external world and other people.

Although we have dominant characteristics, these are not necessarily fixed. People also adapt their personality in different situations and with different people. For example an introvert working in a job that requires extroversion may decide to be more social because it's important for their career development. Or, for example an extrovert who is leading a team might decide to take time out from giving orders to instead listen to staff.

So what can we learn about ourselves when we understand which side of the personality fence we are sitting on? And how does this influence our career choices, relationships and overall lifestyle?

Extroverts

An extrovert is usually the first to speak up. If you ask a question and the person immediately responds and seems to be thinking out loud. Then there is a good chance that they have an extroverted personality. If after asking a question the person takes a second or two to respond. Then there is a good chance that they have an introverted personality type.

Human connection has a greater influence on extroverts than introverts. In fact, it has been proven that the brains of extroverts respond more to photos of humans faces than compared to neutral photos of nature. An extrovert will confide in anyone, they speak more and often have a big circle of friends. However the connections are not particularly strong.

In working environments extroverts perform well in careers involving direct interaction with people and team based efforts. They enjoy working in open spaces, are quick decision makers and enjoy lots of attention. However they are easily distracted. Some examples are of jobs perfect for extraverts are events, police officer, musician and entertainer.

One of the most famous extraverts is Bill Clinton. The former President of the United States of America was always full of energy. Clinton thrived in publicity and energized people through speeches and meetings. To both friends and opponents he will be remembered as, outgoing, social and friendly.

Then we have the famous martial artist, Connor Mcgregor. He calls himself the notorious, the two time champ. He is as famous for his public persona as well as his fighting skills. Mcgregor is a prime example of an extrovert, taunting his opponents with lively rhetoric, as much as his brutal fighting skills. He is flamboyant in the ring, always a showman, and in interviews he is never shy.

Then there is the former British Prime Minister Winston Churchill who had an endless energy, working all hours fueled by whiskey and cigars. Even when he was leading a country at war, he also found energy to write a Nobel Prize winning memoir.

Introverts

Introverts are usually quiet and reserved. They are considered to be more reflective, thinkers who are happy in long periods of solitude. To identify an introvert observe how they recover when stressed or tired. This is a key difference between extroverts and introverts. Introverts tend to withdraw into isolation and sit alone in order to recharge their energy. The more time spent around people in particular large groups of acquaintances will drain their energy. In addition they may also find things such as external noise distracting and will prefer total silence when working. An introvert may only share ideas when prompted.

Age is also a great indicator for reading if someone is introverted or extroverted. As we grow older we tend to calm down and go to more moderate social engagements that require less extroversion.

Brain scans show a more developed prefrontal cortex in introverts which is associated with deeper thinking and planning. This suggests that introverts are less impulsive and prefer to think things over before taking action. However this kind of overthinking makes them more susceptible to depression and anxiety.

Introverts tend to prefer more deep conversation and appreciate listening to others. Give them plenty of space during conversations and respect their time. They will want to know that they are being understood. If they feel your not interested in what they have to say then they will likely leave. If you want to make a real connection with them then listen with care and interest. Also be sure to respond authentically and in depth. If you're an extrovert talking to an introvert make sure to give them enough time to respond after you say something.

All of this doesn't mean to say that introverts are antisocial. They will often appreciate being in contact with others. It just depends on with whom and for how long. Introverts are just as capable as extroverts of applying social skills. They will likely manage their interactions in a more disciplined way with a defined schedule. Its less likely for them to indulge in social activities as a form of escapism. Time is also an important factor in the decision making process of introverts. Often pressuring them for a decision is a bad strategy. Introverts will make their best decisions with time and solitude.

Jobs that allow a person to working independently are a good fit for introverts. Introverts prefer working in quiet spaces and don't need praise. They tend to ponder decision-making more carefully and are good at focusing for long periods of time. Ideal jobs for introverts include, graphic design, software development, taxi driver and more.

On of the famous introverts is Bill Gates, the founder of technology giant Microsoft. He is well known for being incredibly focused which has allowed him to spend thousands of working on complicated tasks. He has talked about having to learn some extravert skills due to the demands of running such a huge company.

Perhaps one of the most surprising introverts is Michael Jordan. You might think that sports is all about being extroverted. But Jordan was well known for being reclusive. Preferring to spend long periods of time alone recharging and perfecting his game.

Then there is Facebook founder and CEO Mark Zuckerberg. He is known as being shy and introverted. To people that don't know him he comes off as cold and reserved. But he does genuinely care about the people working with him and excels working for long periods of time alone.

What about relationships, is there an ideal match up?

Often it's difficult for extroverts to truly understand introverts. Conflict could be caused because the extrovert wishes to go out and be social whereas the introvert will likely prefer to stay home. Extroverts may become upset with their partner for being antisocial and not talking with people. The extrovert may well encourage the introvert socialize, but this might be perceived as being too pushy and not accepting them. The introvert may feel that the extrovert never listens and speaks too much.

There are clearly many differences between introverts and extroverts. Being an introvert or extrovert is neither better or worse than the other. Most people have both aspects integrated into their personality and sit naturally between the two. They are commonly known as ambiverts who have a personality type that doesn't lean heavily in either direction. As a result they have a much easier time adjusting to various situations which helps them to connect more easily with a wider variety of people.

The Masks People Wear

People wear masks to hide their real identity, emotions and feelings. The world can be a tough place and a natural response is to hide behind a mask. Social pressure, abuse and harassment cause people to mask their normal personality. This can be at the cause of strong influences such as parents, rejection and physical or emotional abuse. Sometimes the habit of wearing a mask runs so deep that the individual might not even be aware of their masking.

Many of us wear masks in our career, others in socializing or daily living and so on. A person could be feeling terrible on the inside but hide it with a big smile. Sometimes we feel obligated to wear a mask because you have to hide the truth from others. This is really commonplace in work and environments with hierarchy.

People go to great lengths to attain social acceptance. Pretending to be confident. Faking humour, gossiping and so on. Sometimes when we are insecure we might lie and make things up. Or when we don't feel loved we can mask that with anger. We pretend things are fine, even when they are not.

Many of us hide who we truly are through these masks. We hide from our loved ones and ultimately from ourselves. Some people have put on so many masks that they have lost themselves and the essence of who they truly are.

A lot of these behaviors are the result of our childhood experiences that later shape us. Not many of us emerge from childhood with a fresh attitude. We unconsciously and consciously adopt certain behavioural patterns to seek stability and security in our lives. These are our masks and protect us from shame and hurt. Here are some of the masks we wear.

Avoidance Mask

Sensitive individuals and sufferers of anxiety often try to hide their real self behind an avoidance mask to avoid all the pain. Imposter syndrome is one of the most common reasons for wearing masks. We fear that everyone is going to find us out. They are going to find out that all along we are a fake. But being yourself without that mask is fine. We need to live into our potential.

Functional Mask

A Functional Mask is the type people wear at work to look competent. Consider famous people who don't want to show their emotions to the tabloids as an example. In this regard you still feel your emotions but shield them from others temporarily.

Mask of Anger

Anger can be a protection mechanism to avoid getting hurt. Angry people often cover up their sensitivities in this way. On the other hand some might mask that with happiness. Joking and smiling all the time to hide their anxieties and insecurity.

The Calm

Looking from the outside this person appears to be calm and collected in all situations. Conflicts and chaos don't rattle them. But behind the mask they bottle up emotions which often boil over into nervous breakdowns and snapping at people.

The Humorist

Humour is a powerful defense mechanism. However it does prevent intimacy. Especially sarcasm which is usually rooted in pain. The humorist tends to avoid serious conversations by cracking jokes and will be uncomfortable with conflict. Their comedy serves as a protective shield.

The Overachiever

Some strive to achieve perfectionism as a defense mechanism against their world falling apart. Accolades and praise may provide some temporary relief but they are always at the mercy of things going wrong. The result is that the are in a perpetual state of anxiety. In addition the associated stubbornness and obsessiveness makes it difficult for them to build trust and intimacy with loved ones.

The Martyr

The Martyr believes they have a critical role in the world and rationalizes their selfless actions in this regard. These exaggerations often drive people away.

The Bully

Most of us are familiar with bullies. From the schoolyard to the workplace we often encounter the bully. The bully will try to assert control over others from gentle manipulation to more aggressive or even physical intimidation. Bullies may appear to be confident and powerful but their manipulation often stems from insecurities and self doubt. They feel the need to demand respect as a way of gaining value.

The Control Freak

Control freaks are fearful of ambiguity. They use order and exertion of power in an attempt to achieve a sense of security. They are usually over caring for all of those around them even when they are quite fine. When others deviate from plans they become agitated.

Self Loathing

Self loathing individuals project a negative view of themselves and are at the mercy of their own insecurities. This makes it difficult for them to be intimate with others. In some ways they see this as a protective mechanism from getting hurt.

The People Pleaser

People pleasers have their sense of value based on the opinion of others and will go to great lengths to win approval from them. They lack a strong foundation and will seek advice from others. They are also easily influenced by the opinions of others and will do whatever it takes to make others happy. Their own preferences, thoughts or feelings are suppressed as a result.

The Introvert

Introverts would much rather be lonely then risk failure or rejection. Just like the perfectionist they are afraid of making mistakes so avoid challenges. They are embarrassed easily and avoid saying much in order to avoid being wrong.

The Social Butterfly/Extravert

Social butterflies might appear to be the life and soul of the party but they are often lonely and empty on the inside. They compensate for their feelings of insecurity with small talk and fleeting experiences. Often they will have many people around them and a busy social calendar but most of those so called friendships are lacking in depth. Conversations are kept superficial to avoid revealing anxieties. Relationships are also shallow and promiscuity is common.

The Myers-Briggs Type, Indicator (MBTI)

The Myers-Briggs Type, Indicator (MBTI) is an excellent tool for reading people and understanding relationships. MBTI explains cognition which is how people process information. These are the four basic modes of cognition that every person has. Those are sensing, intuition, thinking and feeling. These four modes also exist in two orientations either introverted or extroverted and these combinations form the eight cognitive functions.

Note that extraverted used with these terms means anything happening external to your mind. This is in the real world, in real time. When you see the word introverted it means what goes on on the inside. That can be past present or future.

The human brain takes in information through perceiving and then makes decisions through judging. Perceiving is the process of taking in information from the external world and compiling it in our minds. Judging is the process of evaluating that information based on either internal or external criteria.

When you understand about cognitive functions and personality types it will help you to read people.

Perceiving Functions

There are four ways to take in information which are known as perceiving functions. Those are:

Extraverted Sensing (Se):
spontaneous, adaptable, optimistic and adventurous

Extroverted sensing involves experiencing the world around you in the form of sights, sounds and sensations. The process happens in the present moment. Extroverted sensors tend to notice much more details and respond faster than others. They also learn very quickly from experiences. They excel at noticing data from experiences and then making practical use of the knowledge. They also seek to understand the world around them and participate in it. As such they are energized from direct interaction with the outside world such as people, nature and events.

Introverted Sensing (Si):
Reliable, routine, clear and attentive

Introverted sensors draw on past experiences to understand the present and future. They pay close attention to detail and use this to quickly problem solve and make decisions. Sensing introverted involves remembering experiences in detail and comparing them to other experiences to in turn find similarities. These are individuals who are focused on their inner, subjective world of personal experiences.

They tend to have a strong intuition, self regulation and awareness. This makes them great at coming up with solutions. In their personal lives they prefer consistency and loyalty. As a result they often will have the same set of friends or relationships for their life.

Extraverted Intuiting (Ne):
Inspiring, impatient, imaginative, charismatic

Extraverted Intuitors are good at identifying relationships between things and finding hidden meanings behind things. They view everything as being connected and having many possibilities. However living in a world of multiple possibilities can make them unsure of their conclusions or cause them to have trouble deciding. Primarily they tend to be focused on the future and seeing the bigger picture. To many they are inspiring but often get stuck in the monotony of day to day life. They like to express new ideas and possibilities with great enthusiasm, often jumping from ideas. This makes them great entrepreneurs since they prefer to innovate and work well in chaos.

Introverted Intuiting (Ni):
Individualistic, strategic, mysterious, creative

Introverted intuitors are very good at noticing patterns, relationships between things and how they fit into a larger picture. They tend to find meaning in abstract concepts. As a result they are great at solving problems and planning for the future. They are always looking forward to the future and are less concerned with present circumstances. Primarily they are focused on their inner subjective world which they seek to connect with the outer world. They tend to work well withdrawn from external stimulation and can be quite unpredictable but very insightful. Often they will seem very detached from their environment and come across as daydreamers. For them it is difficult to explain their insights and they are often slow to reply because they get frustrated when explaining themselves. Abstract art or music are better ways for them to explain.

Judging Functions

There are four ways we make decisions which are known as judging functions. We use the judging functions when making decisions. Remember, everyone uses both thinking and feeling, but some prioritize one over the other. Those are:

Extraverted Thinking (Te):
leader, attention to detail, confident, strict

Extraverted thinkers are very good at organizing and efficiency. When they decide to accomplish a goal they're very good at finding potentially successful solutions. They may come off as authoritative but in reality they are trying to do there best to make things work. Primarily they focus on logical judgments to organize and evaluate information in the outer world.

Emotionally they might seem detached since they are more logical. Ambiguity and indecisiveness frustrate them. In some cases they might rush into decisions too quickly because they want results and are highly goal orientated. Often found working in law, politics and planning.

Introverted Thinking (Ti):
Analytical, honest, smart, logical

Introverted thinking involves organizing, analyzing and evaluating to complete a bigger picture or to better understand things. Introverted thinkers are energized by challenges and troubleshooting. They tend to make decisions based on an internal framework which they are constantly revising and expanding on. Once something has been analyzed and evaluated they will trust in it. As a result they seek perfection and internal order. However they are less likely to share the logic behind when they make a decision and instead prefer privacy. Often they are critical of others and can come across as judgemental. They often look for inconsistencies or flaws mentally try to improve things to reach the best of all possibilities.

Extraverted Feeling (Fe):
Kind, empathetic, sensitive, sincere

Extraverted Feelers focus on the feelings and intentions of other people around them. They are focused on decisions that add value to the

environment, social standards and culture.
Considerate of others and will often put them ahead of
themselves. Their primary motivation is to understand
the values and desires of other people. A healthy does
of extraverted feeling comes across as empathetic and
sincere. Whilst unhealthy dose of if are manipulative
and controlling. They usually are very polite and will
go out of their way to make sure others aren't
embarrassed or hurt and are likely to speak up for
other people. Often involved as leaders for social
causes such as community work, churches and so on.

Introverted Feeling (Fi):
Creative, bold, quiet, open minded

Introverted feelers tend to navigate the world with a
strong system of values and focus on what is right or
wrong. If they sense that their value system has been
broken significantly enough they will have a strong
urge to react. They tend to prefer to express
themselves with feelings and actions rather than
words. Excellent at listening and coming to
conclusions. In life they seek individuality, meaning
and authenticity. However they have an open mind to
other people's values and believe everyone should be
themselves. But they won't tolerate violation of their
rights and aren't afraid to stand up for them.
Discussing their feelings is difficult and they often
privately struggle to be understood. As a result they
are often drawn to art and music as a way of
expressing themselves.

The Enneagram of Personality

The Enneagram of Personality is a concise way of understanding a person's behavior, based on their dominant characteristics and motivators. It is a model used to represent the human psyche and represents it as nine interconnected personality types.

Knowledge of this is a powerful advantage to reading people. It is widely used in business and social contexts to gain insights into interpersonal dynamics. In addition to increasing self awareness and development.

The Enneagram of Personality can indicate people's motivations for the way they act or think. It can also provide insights into relationships with other people. This will help to identify particular strengths, weaknesses and motivations. In the workplace it can help to manage employees more effectively.

Here are some things to consider about The Enneagram of Personality.

- People do not change personality type
- Descriptions are universally applied to females and males

- People fluctuate between the good and bad traits of their personality type.
- Numbers are used to designate types because they are neutral in value. Large or small numbers have no significance
- No type is worse or better than the other

The Enneagram of Personality

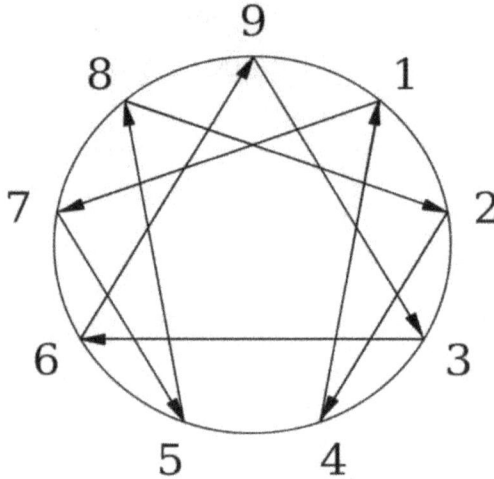

Above is The Enneagram of Personality. It is composed of three parts, an inner triangle (3, 6, 9), an outer circle and a hexagon (1, 4, 2, 8 ,5, 7). The circle is a symbol of unity. The triangle is a symbol of law three and the hexagon is a symbol of law seven.

The nine points around the circumference of The Enneagram of Personality are connected with each other. Each number represents one of the nine distinct personality types. Most of us have a little bit of each of the nine and are more dominant in one of them than others. The one that stands out as being closest to a person is their basic personality type.

To identify someone's basic personality type you need to look at the word clusters for each and choose which they identify closest with. Below are the condensed highlights of each.

Type 1: The Perfectionist
Principled, self controlled, purposeful, perfectionist

The Perfectionist is usually tough on themselves and on other people. They hold everyone, including themselves accountable to higher standards. Normally because of this they are successful and get a lot done in the right way. They want to excel at everything. For them everything has to be perfect and they can sometimes be a control freak.

A strong sense of purpose and internal criticism drives their thoughts and actions. Sometimes they are too self-righteousness and treat others weaknesses with intolerance. However they are dependable and have a lot of self discipline.

Type 2: The Helper
People pleasing, generous, possessive, demonstrative

The Helper is generous, warm, caring and genuinely loves being with other people. They want to be liked. As a result they have many friends who enjoy being around them. They are sensitive to people's needs and are always there to help out. However they also find it hard to say no and as a result are often taken advantage of. This may lead to resentment and bitterness.

Type 3: The Achiever
Adaptable, driven, excelling, image conscious

The Achiever is driven by success and likes to set goals. They tend to excel at everything they do. With others they are charming and inspirational role models. However they fear the opinions of others and try to avoid being low value or low status. As a result they work hard to get the best results and are very efficient. However this can make them a little self centered and oblivious of others feelings.

Type 4: The Individualist
Dramatic, self absorbed, dexpressive, temperamental

The Individualist is self aware, sensitive and experiences emotions on a deeper level. They often spend much time thinking of how things could be. They strive to be unique and are likely to be involved in creative activities. Relationships with them are deep, warm and empathetic.

The challenge for them is frequent bouts of melancholy and self-pity. This can make them emotionally unbalanced and find it hard to work in routine jobs.

Type 5: The Observer
Innovative, perceptive, secretive, isolated

The Observer is a thoughtful and introspective type. They are focused on learning and attaining knowledge. They are not concerned with status or materialism. Instead they are consumed with searching for themselves and prefer privacy. As a result they often are withdrawn from socializing. In addition they tend to focus on logic and distance from emotion. This can make them come across as cold.

Type 6: The Loyalist
Responsible, anxious, engaging, suspicious

The Loyalist focuses on building relationships of trust. At the outset they can be suspicious of others. Quite often they expect the worst case scenario. This makes them doubtful and in need of constant reassurement in order to make themselves feel safer. As a result they are often anxious and can fall into bouts of paranoia or excessive worrying. However they are dependable and will stick to the rules.

Type 7: The Optimist
Versative, scattered, spontaneous, acquisitive

The Optimist is spontaneous and fun who is often in a happy mood. They are pleasure seekers who avoid negativity at all costs. As a result they are less stressed and don't let negative circumstances bother them. They are always looking for the positive side of everything. This can make it challenging for them to commit to things because at the sign of failure they will jump to the next thing before finishing. This usually manifests in promiscuity, prefering to be free rather than being confined to a monogamous relationship. As a result this can make them come across as shallow and impulsive.

Type 8: The Leader
Decisive, self confident, confrontational, willful

The Leader is a strong and dominant type. They depend on nobody and as a result they make great leaders. They will never hesitate to take over control and utilize their strengths to protect others. This can make them confrontational and blunt at times. Others might be offended by their behaviour even if it was not intended by the leader. As a result they are often misrepresented. This can make them come across as intimidating, selfish and even vindictive.

Type 9: The Mediator
Reassuring, receptive, resigned, complacent

The Mediator is an agreeable and complacent character who avoids confrontations. Instead they love to develop healthy relationships with people. They are non-judgmental which makes them good mediators. However their avoidance of conflict can make them withdrawn at times. As a result many are introverts who prefer solitude and live quiet social lives. This can make them indecisive and easily distracted.

Empathy, The Secret To Easily Reading People

Empathy is the ability to understand what a person is feeling and what makes sense to them. Great communication is founded on empathy. Empathy helps us to communicate and read others better. Prosocial behaviour is considered a sign of empathy whereas a lack of empathy is a sign of anti social behaviour. Having empathy is a powerful way of reading people because it helps in understanding the decision making and thought processes of others.

Psychologists and mental health workers are often experts in this regard and they will have a high level of empathy. People who lack in empathy usually make others feel miserable as they are unable to understand others feelings.

For most of us we are wired to be able to feel the emotions that others are feeling. This explains why we cry during sad movies or laugh when others do. Some of us are more a less sensitive to this. However empathy is a skill that can be trained to be better. Depending on your skill level this will be hard or easy practice.

Signs of empathy	Signs of no empathy
Good listener	Argumentative
Overwhelmed by negativity	Defensive
Sensitive	Strong ego
Intuitive	Leader
Caring	Loyal

Psychologists have defined three forms of empathy which all manifest in different ways. Reflect on your home, work and social experiences to notice the different types.

Cognitive Empathy

Cognitive empathy is the awareness of another's perspective or mental state. It can be further subdivided into the following.

- Perspective Taking: A tendency to quickly adopt the psychological perspectives of others.
- Fantasy: Identification with fictional characters.
- Tactical/Strategic Empathy: Deliberate use of perspective taking as a means to achieve results.

Knowing how another person feels and what they might be thinking on an intellectual level is particularly helpful in negotiating and understanding various views. Rather than responding to another's emotions with the same emotion it is the process of responding to them with brain power.

You don't need to embrace the emotions of a sick person to feel for them. Instead, you can understand the parts of the illness. This is a huge advantage when you need to interact with someone tactfully. Particularly negotiations for which emotions don't serve well. Those who have strong cognitive empathy might come across as cold or detached.

Emotional Empathy

Physically feeling in harmony with the other person as though they have passed their emotions to you. This is particularly helpful in close interpersonal relationships such as coaching and management. In some cases it can be overwhelming because it involves directly feeling the emotions of another. People who are masters of emotional empathy are often referred to as an empath. They have the ability to take on the whole emotional or mental state of another. All humans have mirror neurons to make us capable of this. For example when you feel like crying at a wedding or when you see someone hurt it's a natural response to share their emotions.

Compassionate Empathy

The awareness to respond accordingly to another person's mental state. This is linked to being affected by another person's emotion. It can be further subdivided into the following.

- Empathic Concern: Responding with sympathy and compassion for the suffering of others
- Personal Distress: Responding with discomfort and anxiety to another's suffering. This is a self centered form of empathy. However some might argue that it does not constitute empathy.

Everyone should strive for this kind of empathy, to show love for others and care for their outcomes. This is particularly helpful in healthcare where empathy and compassion is felt for the patients. Feelings of the heart and thoughts are intricately connected. Compassionate Empathy honors that natural connection by considering the feelings and mind state of another person. Some of us will focus more on feeling than fixing.

Development of empathy

Basic psychology tells us that people tend to move away from uncomfortable experiences in their childhood as they grow older. For example picture a child who was always one of the weakest kids in school. Maybe he got picked last for the football team or didn't get picked at all. Over time this person developed a long list of painful experiences and emotions. Psychology tells us that this person will seek to move away from pain as they get older. In practice this means the person is likely to pursue things in life that make them appear strong and not weak. For example they might start lifting weights. Or they might run for a powerful position within the government or another organization. Once we understand that people do things to move away from pain we can get a better understanding for why they do the things they do or act in certain ways. This can help us to better empathize with them.

Let's take a look at another example. Picture a small child named Bill, he grew up on the poor side of town and since his parents report he rarely was able to have nice things. When Bill went to school and saw wealthier kids with nicer cars, phones or other materialistic things he experienced a strong sense of pain. While the other kids enjoyed an amazing lunch Bill was lucky if he had anything to eat. Imagine if this continued to happen in every area of Bill's life growing up and how much pain would build up over time. As Bill got older and gained more opportunities one of his main goals in life whether he realized that or not was to move away from the pain of being poor.

Everyone is born with the ability to feel empathy. Compassion and sympathy are often associated with empathy. Compassion can be defined as the emotion we feel for others in need and it motivates us to help. Sympathy can be defined as the feeling to care for someone who is in need. Empathy is often also compared with altruism, especially in the field of positive psychology. Altruistic behaviour is aimed at benefiting another person. Often when someone is showing empathy with another acts of altruism will occur. All of the above should not be confused with pity which is a feeling towards someone in need of help who they cannot help.

From an early age humans start to display the behaviours of empathy. Toddlers have often displayed concerned for others. Empathic development is greatly influenced by parenting style and relationships. That's why it is a good idea to make sure children benefit from social interaction from an early age.

Females tend to have more empathy than males. Women tend to have more awareness of facial expressions and processing emotions. This is likely the result of females being the primary caretakers of children throughout history. In turn this might have led to neurological evolution that has more empathic responses.

Empathy is not just unique to humans. In fact, some animals have more empathy than humans. Species with a more developed prefrontal cortex often have a greater ability to experience empathy. Rodents and monkeys have been shown to demonstrate prosocial behaviour and empathy for others. Most forms of empathy are built on years of evolution.

Communicating with empathy

Empathy increases with similarities in living conditions and culture. It is more likely to occur when individuals are frequently interacting with each other. The knowledge gained from empathy can help you to use the appropriate nonverbal communication.

- **Understand Yourself:**
To understand the emotions of others you first have to learn to empathize with yourself. Through understanding and accepting your own feelings you can build a solid foundation towards empathy with others.

- **Understand Others**
Practicing and committing to thoughtfulness will bring you closer to understanding how others are thinking and feeling. Interacting with someone becomes easy when you understand what they are thinking or feeling.
Understanding the emotional states of people can be achieved by putting yourself into the shoes of the other. To feel their feelings or understand their beliefs and desires. The ability to do that requires sophisticated imagination which can be trained.

A successful empathic interaction involves accurate recognition of the other person's ongoing emotional states and thought processes. Accurate recognition of those are foundational pillars of empathy. On a basic level humans have the ability to recognize others feelings through body language and facial expressions. Vocal tonality is also a way to tune into empathy.

Individuals acting in an empathetic manner will tend to focus on the long term welfare of others rather than any short term solutions. Empathetic attitudes can be used to improve groups associated with stigma such as the ill, different races, convicts and so on.

Part Two: Clues To Reading People

There are a number of things that you can pay attention to in order to effectively read people. All of us are different but at the core we are the same and everyone gives away clues about themselves all the time. Everytime you interact with people they are sending you clues and signs that you need to watch out and listen for. Awareness of other people's emotions and thoughts will help to improve your interpersonal relationships.

The first step to take is to improve your own self-awareness. However remember don't get that confused with being overly self conscious to the extent that you constantly worry about what others think. That will only lead to base level conversations without depth. Instead try to increase your observational skills and focus your attention onto others. Ideally you want to be looking at everyone without judgement and know when you are having opinions about other people. When you can easily identify your own emotions it will help to reveal what is the driving force of different emotions. Then you can start to predict and see them in other people. In turn this will help you to realize when conversations are going well or not.

Practice makes perfect making predictions about how a conversation is going. When your out and about practice observing conversations. Does that girl like that guy? Who is the leader in the group? Or take the time out and watch a foreign film. Pay close attention to the way the characters interact to see if you can notice anything interesting. After a few movies you'll become a pro at this and your observation skills will become much better. That kind of practice is going to help you become really good at reading people. But the truth of all of this is you have to go out and be scientific about it. Because essentially your predicting patterns and once you start to apply it to your own life it will stick.

That is how you can become much, much better at reading people and learning what triggers them. In turn you can be more captivating and more interesting. You have to get great at noticing the world around you and not the world within you.

Now, let's take a look at some of the clues people give away. Remember to always ask questions that are open ended. This will give you more feedback to analyze and allow you to observe people for longer. Watch out for and listen to their responses.

The Clues

Baseline

Get to know the person you are reading. This will give you a better idea of who they are and how they behave. If you have the opportunity, form opinions of them based on multiple encounters with them.

There are particular mannerisms and habits that everyone has which are unique to them. Everyone has a personal blueprint, showing how they walk, sit, and stand. Establish their baseline. This is their normal relaxed state. Observe how they behave in this state.

To find this out, begin by getting them into a relaxed state. Take the time necessary to create calm, use small talk and low pressure topics or questions. Ask, pause and then observe. Make sure you are posing questions and allowing adequate time for their responses. Try not to overwhelm them with rapid fire questions. Make the questions specific to elicit the kind of information you want. Keep the line of questioning relevant and focused.

Note how they look normally, how they sit, their hand placement, their usual feet position, posture, common facial expressions, head tilt, and even where they place or hold their possessions. Do they take long strides when walking? How do they hold their head? Is their body language open or closed off?

Observe and remember these. When you have an understanding of someone's baseline you will easily notice any differences.

Difference

Once you have established a baseline look for inconsistencies. For example a normally attentive person who seems distracted probably has something going on. Once you understand how they normally behave you will notice things that stick out. Changes in the behaviour of a person signal changes in their thoughts and emotions. Consider when we get bad news, our bodies will reflect that change of emotions. With careful observation we can notice any changes in behaviour.

When there is a different kind of behaviour, it is usually a sign that the line of questioning, stimulus or an event that is troubling the person. Our bodies manifest discomfort in pacifiers. When we are scared, nervous, or uncomfortable this can manifest as fidgeting, touching the face, sweating, breathing heavily and so on. Remember these do not necessarily indicate deception. They could for example indicate that the person is uncomfortable. Liars will often use objects to build a barrier between you and them. This is a sign that they want distance because they are uncomfortable or are being deceitful. Or when people are uncomfortable they tend to lean away.

Determine the cause of the pacifying behaviours. It might not necessarily be that a person is lying but it could be a sign of stress. Go deeper and find the reasons. With effective questioning it is possible to get a better read of people.

Clusters

Always read people in clusters. Behaviours that occur in succession are known as clusters and are the parts of a puzzle to reading people. The more pieces of the puzzle you have then the better chance you have to complete the full picture.

Deciphering singular actions or movements usually doesn't give away much information about a person. But when they happen together with several other movements it will reveal much more about them. Don't jump to conclusions based off of one clue. Take in the whole picture of their, words, tonality, body language and so on. More on that later.

It's important to consider that there is not one way or method that can be applied to every single person. We have to take into account people's culture, family background, environment, mental health and other internal factors. However people do generally follow some patterns in speech, thoughts and body language. These are implicit behaviours such as anxious nail biting, bored foot tapping, avoiding eye contact and so on. Again though try to consider the factors of the person before making assumptions.

Comfort and Discomfort

Observe whether someone is comfortable or not. This is a key indicator to how well an interaction is going. If they are showing signs of being uncomfortable then maybe you need to pull back. Otherwise you can pursue the line of conversation and perhaps go deeper.

People who are comfortable will tend to have more open body language, showing more of their torsos, insides of their arms and legs. A good sign of comfort between people is synchrony in their nonverbal behavior. That is shown in similar breathing rhythm, vocal tonality and body language or posture. On the other hand when people are sitting differently or having different tonality then that is a sign of discomfort

Other signs of discomfort include, a mouth squirming, a frown, an overly long facial expression, rubbing the forehead or neck, squeezing the face, stroking the back of the head, fidgeting and eyelid flutter. If they are noticeably sweating and having trouble to breath then it is an obvious sign of discomfort. Listen to their voice which will likely crack or mumble when someone is in discomfort.

Intuition

Many of us are under the false belief that trusting your instincts is just a cult practice or phenomenon. But there is real science behind it. Emotions originate from the brain and are communicated to our facial and bodily expressions. Those give away so much and intuition picks up on them.

The feelings you have when you first meet someone are usually a powerful indicator of sensing what kind of a person they are. This is your intuition and it is what your gut feels. When you read someone with your intuition it allows you to see deeper than the obvious.

To practice using intuition there are three things that you must pay attention to.

• **Honor your gut feelings**
A gut feeling is your body perceiving information before your brain has the time to think about it. It's a primal response. You can think of it like your internal truth meter and it will help you determine if you can trust a person or not. Be aware of it especially when you first meet someone.

• **Take notice if you get goose bumps**
These are the intuitive tingles that tell you when someone inspires or moves you. Goose bumps are also caused when someone says something that really

tugs at your character. It is a positive sign that this person is good for you.

- **Pay close attention to flashes of insight**
If you've ever had an aha moment during a conversation where you felt like you really got a feel for the person's true character then this was your intuition at work. These flashes of insight happen so quickly so they can get lost in the chatter if you're not paying attention to them.

Moving forward there are many, many more clues that we give away in our nonverbal behaviours, our words and even the way we behave online. Let's take a look at those.

Nonverbal Communication

Nonverbal communication is a key indicator to reading people. Most people are unaware of the information they are communicating nonverbally or how to read it. Incidentally over ninety percent of communication is conveyed using non verbals. In fact, it is quite hard to have a successful interaction without nonverbals. This is the reason why people often fly to meetings in the age of, text and emails. Nothing can come close to seeing nonverbals up close and personal.

Body Language

Sometimes the words we say are different from how we really feel. Body language is more difficult to fake. We give off a lot of information through our bodies, mannerisms and gestures. Therefore body language is one of the most trustworthy ways of reading a person.

Body language is the main nonverbal communication and is achieved through gestures, facial expressions, touching, posture, movements, accessories and clothing. Learning to read body language is a valuable skill towards successfully reading people. These can be actions such as eye contact, positioning and more.

Eye Contact

People have always said the eyes are the windows into the soul and if we're talking about a person's true personality then there's a lot of truth to this. Like the entire body itself the eyes transmit powerful electromagnetic energy and if you take the time to observe a person's eyes you can see if they are angry, happy, distracted and more.

When you communicate with someone observe their eye contact. Are they making direct eye contact or are they constantly looking away? A lack of direct eye contact is an indicator of boredom or even deceit. If they look down that can indicate submission or nervousness. Dilated pupils are a great indicator of interest. Our pupils dilate as a result of increased cognitive effort which essentially means more focus on you.

If they glance at something such as the door, that could indicate that they want to leave. Looking upwards or to the left is often a signal of lying. Whereas when people look to the right its coming from imagination.

The rate at which someone blinks is another indicator of how to read people. When blinking rate increases its usually the result of a person being stressed out. In some cases it also indicates lying and it's especially obvious when combined with touching of the face.

Face

When you pay close attention to someone's facial expressions you can pick up on some key non verbal indicators. Specifically, the first thing you should start to do is identifying your own expressions.

Psychological research has concluded that there are six universal facial expressions. These correspond to distinct universal emotions: happiness, sadness, surprise, fear, disgust, anger.

- Happiness: raising of the mouth corners and wrinkling of the eyes. A happy smile fills the whole face.
- Sadness: lowering of the mouth corners, facial features drop.
- Surprise: eyebrows arch, eyes wide open, paler complexion, jaw drop.
- Fear: eyebrows raised, eyes wide open, mouth open
- Disgust: upper lip raised, bridge of nose wrinkled, raised cheeks
- Anger: eyebrows lowered, pressed lips, bulging eyes, flushed complexion.

Pay close attention to the mouth. There are various types of smiling, from the genuine to the fake. Genuine smiles use the whole face and indicate that a person is happy. Fake smiles use only the mouth and are used to seek approval or to establish comfort. Half smiles are usually indicators of sarcasm or uncertainty. A mouth with tight, pursed lips usually is an indicator of displeasure. Whilst a relaxed mouth indicates a more positive and relaxed mood. When someone covers or touches their mouth it may be an indicator of lying or deception.

Finally, the details of a person's face can reveal a lot about their personality. Frown lines on the bridge of the nose or forehead are an indicator of someone who often worries. Whilst wrinkles around the corners of the eyes likely indicate someone more relaxed who smiles and laughs often.

Head Movement

Take note of head movements. When the head moves in harmony upwards with positive statements then this is a sign of congruence in emotion and behaviour. However opposites are more likely to be the result of lies and deception. For example nodding the head upwards when making negative statements.

How quickly or slowly a person nods their head is an indicator of patience. Someone who nods slowly when you talk is indicating patience and a wish for you to continue. Whilst someone who nods quickly when you talk to them is indicating that they want you to hurry up. If they tilt their head to the side when you talk then that can be a sign of interest. Tilting the head backwards can be a sign of suspicion or unease. When people are interested in others they will point their head at them. Take a look at group interactions to determine who is the leader.

Feet

People are often so focused on controlling their facial expressions and upper body positioning that they leak important non verbal messages through their feet. This might sound ridiculous but you can tell a lot about people through their feet. Particularly in hierarchy. When people are in groups you can tell who is the leader by who has the most feet pointed towards them. Or in one on one situations when people have their feet pointed towards you it is an indication of rapport. But if their feet are pointing towards someone else then it's likely they would rather talk to them.

Hands and Arms

Just like the feet the hands also leak important nonverbal cues. Observe where people put their hands. Pockets in hands or touching of head can indicate nervousness or deception. People tend to point their hands towards the person they share the most affinity with. Hands supporting the head with elbows on a table is an indicator of boredom. Hands on hips indicated a sign of exerting dominance. Crossed arms are usually seen as defensive and a closed mind. However with a smile and relaxed demeanor it will indicate confidence and relaxed attitude. When people are holding something whilst communicating it is an indicator of discomfort or unease.

Mirroring

When we are in rapport with someone we often mimic or mirror their emotions and body language. Observing when this happens can give you many clues about how another person is feeling.

Mirroring involves copying the other person's body language, imitating gestures and speech patterns. This can work particularly well in situations such as job interviews or dates. Check to see if the other person is mirroring your behaviour. Change up your body movements and posture and see if they do the same. If someone follows what you do then this is a good sign that they are trying to establish rapport with you.

Mirroring occurs mostly as a subconscious act and often goes unnoticed by both people engaged in communication. Mirroring allows people to feel more connected with whoever they communicate with and establishes better rapport. In conversations listeners will often smile or frown in harmony with the speaker in addition to matching their body posture and movement.

Establishing rapport is an important part of a quality social life. Mirroring can help massively in that regard. This will lead others to believe one is more similar to them and would be a great friend, partner or colleague. In addition mirroring individuals of higher power can create an illusion of higher status. This is particularly advantageous for people that are bargaining with more powerful people.

Proximity

Proximity is the distance between you and the person your communicating with. This can determine if they view you favorably or not. Observe how near or far someone is away from you. When someone stands or sits close to you then it is an indicator of good rapport. However if the rapport is not great they will usually back up or move away from you.

When you see people communicating you can determine a lot about their relationship based on their distance from each other. Although this can also be a cultural thing. Some cultures prefer close proximity whilst others prefer more distance. Always be aware of your location and situation.

Appearance

A person's outer appearance can give away many clues about them.

Clothing

Observe how people dress. Quality of fabrics, brands and styles may reflect status and income level. Logos and fashion choices are good indicators of income. Those who wear fashionable brands are usually on a higher income. Whereas those wearing older generic clothes tend to be on lower incomes. People who constantly follow fashion trends are usually more self conscious and concerned about what others think. T-shirts and attire with other cities and destinations are likely to indicate that the person is well travelled.

A person's shoes can tell you their emotions, political affiliation, income, gender and even age. Expensive shoes tend to belong to high-income earners. Colorful, flashy shoes belong to extroverts. Shoes that aren't new but look spotless belong to conscientious personalities. Functional or practical shoes belong to agreeable people. Ankle boots can be associated with people with an aggressive personality. Shoes that look uncomfortable belong to people with a calm personality. Well-kept and brand new shoes belong to people who often are anxious. Less expensive shoes or flip-flops to belong to liberal thinkers. Plain, boring shoes belong to people who don't care what others think of them and have difficulty forming relationships.

Grooming

A well groomed person is usually conscientious. That would be reflected in a well maintained appearance. Neat hairstyles, trimmed facial hair, ironed and clean clothes. A healthy does of this is normal. Anything less and the person is usually suffering from low self esteem or lower income.

In extreme cases where people pay too much attention to grooming they might well be suffering from obsessive compulsive disorder. In addition, the more people value grooming the higher their ego and income tends to be.

Tattoos and Modifications

Accessories, piercings, tattoos and jewelry can reveal a lot about someone's belief systems, personality, family history, hobbies and interests.

Gang members often have specific tattoos to show their allegiance. People who have been in prison also often have distinctive tattoos. But not all tattoos have negative connotations. They might be related to loved ones or to show a persons artistic side. If someone has a larger tattoo or one in a very noticeable place that usually indicates them as being a nonconformist.

Modifications are things such as piercings, surgery and implants. These also give us important clues about a person. A woman who enhances her breasts will usually do so for confidence reasons. Likewise a man who has liposuccion is trying to increase his value in the sexual marketplace. In the same regard as tattoos the more noticeable the modification the more it gives away about a person. More extreme modifications are often the result of self esteem issues and difficulty relating with people. These people will be more sensitive to communicate with.

Word Clues

The words people say can tell you a lot about them. Choice of words are the result of values, desires, thoughts and concerns. One can get closer to understanding another person by observing the words they speak or write. Behavioral characteristics are revealed through the choice of certain words. Even the way someone texts can reveal many things about their personality.

When we think we use verbs and nouns. Then when speaking, adjectives, adverbs and other grammatical elements are added to turn thoughts into speech or writing. The most basic sentence is constructed with a subject and a verb. For example.

- *"I walked"*
- *"We ate"*
- *"She listened"*

Words added to this structure modify the noun or the action of the verb. It is these modifications that provide key insights into the mind of the speaker or writer.

Using word clues allows us to analyze a person's character. As an example, if someone frequently uses the word "quickly" it would be reasonable to assume that they have a sense of urgency. Conscientious people tend to see themselves as being reliable with a sense of urgency. They might walk "quickly" to avoid being late for work. Or work "quickly" to meet an important deadline. People with this kind of character would make a great employee and this explains the usefulness of listening for word clues. Here are some more examples of word clues.

"I worked hard"
The word "hard" suggests this person values things that are difficult to achieve. It also suggests that they can delay gratification or believe that hard work produces good results.

"I waited patiently"
The use of the word "patiently" suggests this is a person who adheres to social norms and etiquette. They will respect authority follow the rules.

"I love it"
The use of the word "love" suggests this is a person who values family and relationships. They are someone who can be trusted and relied on.

Repetition

Does the person frequently repeat certain words?

"I can't complain about that"
"She makes me happy"
"I'm thrilled to go there"

The above might appear to be quite unrelated statements. However when you look closer you will notice that the word "happy" or one of its synonyms is mentioned in each of the statements. This person is likely to have a positive mindset and will tend to choose things that will make them the most "happy".

When someone is being deceptive they are less likely to use first person pronouns. For example a truthful person might say, "I paid all of the bills", whereas a deceptive one might say "the bills are paid."

People who use "I" more often tend to be more relatable, kind and truthful. Whist those who use "I" at less often tend to be more confident. In addition high status people will use the word "I" the least. People with lower lowest status tends to use the word "I" more often.

Swearing or obscenity significantly increase the persuasiveness of speech and the perceived intensity of the speaker. However it has no effect on their credibility.

A couple's use of the word "we" can predict a satisfying relationship. Use of the word "we" indicates a healthy relationship whereas the use of "you" words suggests problems.

Tonality

Tonality is another important clue to reading people. Consider telephone calls. You can instantly detect the mood of the other person on the telephone. Pay close attention when you listen to someone speak. Is their pitch high or low? How loud do they speak?

There are numerous characteristics of tonality voice that give meaning to a message. These include, timbre, volume, speed, clarity and projection. Different tones can convey different meanings, this can even help in a foreign language. Your tone communicates a lot more than you realized. Essentially, this is the musical notes that your voice communicates separated from your words. Maybe you have a frustrated tone of voice. Maybe you have an angry tone of voice. Maybe you have a warm welcoming tone of voice. Ask yourself. What does this communicate to the people around me? You want to make sure you're sending off the right nonverbals to accompany your words.

A deep voice tone is a sign of maturity and trust in other people. Firm, confident voices convey importance whilst quiet voices convey weakness of uncomfortable. If you want to know who the leader of that group is to listen for the person who speaks with the strongest voice. Some will be loud, some will be very soft but one voice will sound stronger than the rest and this is the leader of the group. This is the easiest way to find a leader of any group and is also a great way to project confidence and become the leader.

The next time that you're walking through the mall or the store or even when around friends or family consciously pay attention to the strength of each person's voice. A strong voice is a good sign that they probably also have a strong personality. a weak voice is a good sign that they probably have a weak personality.

Reading People Online

On a conscious and subconscious level we are constantly judging people. This also occurs online. But in this regard we are judging a prepared set of information that shows people what the user wants them to see about themselves.

A person's interests, relationship status, group membership, photos and written vocabulary can help you form valid impressions of their personality. Usually profiles reveal truths we can't always access from meeting someone in person. This is important because if you like someone based on their social media profile then you will probably like them in real life. Therefore creating an online profile with best portrayal of you for someone to positively judge you is essential.

Social media is a revolutionary way of connecting people who might not meet in the real world. This is of particular benefit to introverted people or those with social anxiety.

Profile Picture

Imagine if you could read a person's personality just by looking at their profile picture on social media. In fact you can discover a lot about a person from their profile picture.

People who score higher for neuroticism tend to have simple photos with less color. These people are also more likely to display a blank expression in their photos. Extroverted individuals usually have a profile picture with other people in it. The images are more likely to be colorful and show the person smiling. If the majority of the pictures you post are of you alone then you might come off as conceited. People who have the best-looking profile pictures are most likely to be open to experience and have pictures with a higher contrast. Highly agreeable people are usually smiling and the pictures look lively and bright.

Comments

The way people phrase comments can give away a lot about their personality and the way they treat others. To make sure your making the best impression of yourself say your comments out loud before you post them. Most people are way more harsh online than in the real world. Which can lead to an inaccurate portrayal of them.

Too much negativity can cause our own thinking to be negative and other people's opinions can influence our own. In fact other peoples comments can also influence whether we perceive something as being true or false. When we lack information we are more likely to seek and trust other people's opinions, regardless of accuracy. Numerous studies conclude that when people see more positive posts it influences them to create more positive posts and comments. The same is true with negative posts and comments.

People tend to value receiving comments more highly than likes. Reading comments can even influence how we behave online. That can cause groups or mob like behaviour to form around and idea. Primarily the beginning comment will influence the following negative or positive tone of the comment thread. If it is a positive first comment then positivity will follow. Whilst negative first comments trigger a chain reaction of negativity. On a conscious and subconscious level other people influence and the way we post.

Comments are perceived as social support whilst likes are less personalised. Whereas likes are less personalised and are just a small hit. Most people online users are passive and just consume information without participating. Users who frequently comment on news articles are mostly lower level educated and lower income men. Trolls, or those who frequently post offensive comments tend to have narcissistic, psychopath personalities. Therefore take comments with a grain of salt.

Behaviour varies on platforms. Those where people use their real names are more likely to behave politely. Whereas platforms with anonymity have much more rude comments and personal insults. If your posting very opinionated things then it could damage your reputation. Especially if it is coming from a professional or public account such as Linkedin.

Behaviour

Social media is an extension of human personality. Various studies have determined that social media is connected to a person's mental health, intellect and more. Research has even found that depression is caused by people who frequently browse social media. People who are more self absorbed tend to be more active online, frequently posting and so on. This can directly increase their feelings of importance and confidence. All those likes, follows and shares give a confidence boost that can be addictive. Their values are based on it.

Every time you post something on social media it might be revealing more about you that you want. The way we behave on social media is linked closely to our attachment style, which affects everything from partner selection to relationship development. Recognizing attachment style helps to identify strengths and weaknesses in relationships. It is also a baseline indicator of a person's capacity for intimacy and success in relationships. Those with insecurity in attachment are less likely to be involved in social media and social networks. They may also drive people away.

The big five personality traits in particular, agreeableness, conscientiousness and neuroticism are closely linked with social network addiction. People strong in neuroticism have more chance of being hooked on social media. Whilst conscientiousness people have a decreased chance of being a social media addict. Agreeableness and conscientiousness are also more likely to be addicted to social media. Because friendly, conscientious people will actively spend more time engaging on social media to keep in touch with friends and family to nourish their network. Extroverts are more likely to post about social events and have pictures with people. Those low in agreeableness are likely to gossip about others online.

Presenting a socially desirable and positive self is a natural occurrence for people online. However if your always painting your life to be perfect then you might well push people away. We all have struggles in life and if you don't share them it might well make you not be relatable. If you paint the perfect life it's not really authentic. It might well be as average as the rest of your social media friends. Just give a good mix of the ups and downs to stay relatable. In addition avoid posting too often about every single moment of your life.

<u>Cold Reading</u>

Cold reading is a popular people reading technique used to obtain and imply a knowledge of someone through using high probability guesses. The method works most effectively in one to one communication.

The first step towards a successful cold read is to make sure that the person is compliant. A successful cold read relies on reinforcing assumptions and quickly moving on from wrong assumptions. Depending on the subjects replies dictates whether or not you should pursue further any promising answers or abandon those that are not.

The technique of shotgunning is most commonly used in cold reading. The reader fires a cluster of assumptions and questions in the hope that one or more will hit the target. The subject will reply to confirm or deny information suggested by the reader and this forms the line of communication.

Accurate reads will lead into much deeper territories because the subject will ponder on how the reader could know such things. Expert cold readers emphasize this by hanging on to those successful hits whilst quickly moving on from any misses.

Look out for subtle clues in body language, differences, pacifiers and tonality to determine if a line of enquiry is successful or not. With practice and improved ability to read people, it is possible to quickly read signals and assume whether the cold read is going in the correct direction.

Open ended statements that seem personal yet can apply to many people give the reader a maximum chance of being correct. These statements can be reinterpreted by the subject in a number of ways and will usually make them eager to fill in details or make connections. Essentially they will elicit responses from the subject to correct or provide more accurate responses which reveal a great deal of information to the assumptions.

For example, "I sense you are quite shy with strangers" or "you had an accident involving water when you were a child" or "your having problems with relatives". Or for example, most people wear jewelry related to the loss of a loved one. But if they are asked about it in the context of a cold read then the subject might be shocked that the reader could know that. Successful cold reading makes the reader appear gifted when in reality the statements could fit most people.

Assumptions and statements can also be used to decipher personality traits. Again the reader would present open ended general statements. This is very successful because personality is not quantifiable and nearly everybody has a mix of personality traits. For example "most of the time you are positive and happy" or "your humble and kind person". Cold readers can choose from a variety of personality traits and then use them together with the opposite in order to elicit a response which they can then probe further.

Notable performers such as Derren Brown have openly used cold reading techniques. But only after acclaim and praise did they reveal that their sound knowledge of human psychology was the foundation of their success rather than a connection with the occult.

Part Three: Persuasion and Manipulation

Understanding How Persuasion Influences Reading People

Persuasion is a powerful tool both to influence and read people. It can be directed in a positive way to lead people to take actions that will be of benefit to themselves. This in turn will help to make your interactions much more successful.

The purpose of persuasion is to get attention and spark curiosity. After that it is all about arousing their desire to take certain actions. The key component is in convincing them the value of what you are persuading.

Perception of value differs from one person to the next. But you can create perceived value in something simply by influencing the way people perceive it. For example in medicine, a person must believe that it will heal them in order for it to work. Most of the powerful people in the world are all great at persuading people. They can easily influence and change people's beliefs and ideas.

Supply and demand influences market forces and that is based on perception. When you persuade others to perceive you as the best supplier you can in turn create demand. That is essentially marketing.

The best way to persuade people is to create value for them. The greater their perception of your value the more influence you have. Ethically you can then either sell them something great or something not so great. It all depends on how you persuade them.

First of all you need to understand what kind of stimulation the person you are trying to influence responds most to. Kinesthetic, visual or auditory. Awareness of this will make your persuasion tactics more effective. To determine this listen closely to the way they talk. Do they say things like "sounds good" "I see" or "I feel good about that." Those are some of the more obvious examples or people who are more kinesthetic, visual or auditory.

- **Visual**

Those that conceptualize through visual stimulus
"I see, I could picture that"

- **Auditory**

Those that conceptualize through audio stimulus
"I hear you, listen man"

- **Kinesthetic**

Those that conceptualize through felt stimulus
"I feel, i did"

Adjust the way you persuade depending on the kind of person your dealing with. For example if your dealing with a kinesthetic person focus on how they feel. For a visual person focus on imagery. For an auditory focus on the sounds, and so on.

Persuasive Techniques

Mirroring

A powerful persuasion technique is to mirror the body language, posing and positioning of those you communicate with. Try to be subtle with it at first and practice. It might feel a little bit awkward but this will put you into a better rapport with whoever you communicate with. Particularly in interviews this is a great technique to utilize.

In addition, people respond well to those who use similar language. Pay attention to the words people use and incorporate them into your conversations with them. Also pay attention to their speed volume and pitch. Respond similarly. Mastery of mirroring will go a long way to reading people.

Persuasive Words

A number of words that persuasively influence the subconscious exist. These are often used as a call to action.

For example:

"Do it",
"Be this"

Positive words and adjectives are also persuasive.

For example:
"Sure"
"Definitely",
"Certainly"

In addition the following words suggest urgency.

"Now"
"At the moment"

Be aware of how these can be used to persuade people. You can add emphasis when saying them as a part of your conversations to persuade people subconsciously.

Rhetorical Questions

Convince people that they are the ones making decisions when in fact you steered them to this by asking rhetorical questions. Getting people to think for themselves can be very persuasive. It will also give you more information about them and make them more receptive.

For example:

"You didn't think I would say yes to that, did you?"

"Why not?"
"It's hot today, isn't it?"

Eye Contact

Whenever you're communicating with someone eye contact is extremely important to establishing good rapport. Use consistent and non threatening eye contact and it will help you to develop trust. In turn you can be more persuasive.

Emotions

People respond to emotions rather than logic. In order to persuade someone you need to connect with them on an emotional level. According to the greek philosopher Aristotle there are three elements to a persuasion.

- Logic: Logic words and reasons to your argument. Concerns facts and data.
- Ethics: refers to the credibility, knowledge and stature of the person you are trying to persuade
- Emotion: The emotional content, all non thinking motivations that affect decisions and actions. This is the most important element.

In negotiations persuasion will greatly enhance the likelihood of a successful outcome. Have information about yourself ready in publications and so on. This will give you social proof and make you look more credible.

You might consider the use of persuasion techniques to be immoral or dishonest. However you should be aware of them in order to know when you are being manipulated. Now let's take a look at manipulation...

How To Read and Deal With Manipulation

Have you ever felt controlled, regretful or pressured to do something you were not comfortable with? Or it's like you're continually questioning why you do things for people and have certain relationships? You might feel scared, obligated or guilt tripped into doing something that you don't really want to. If so you might be at the cause of manipulation. In fact you probably aren't even aware of it.

Manipulation is a psychological technique used by people to try to control others in order to get what they want. It exploits mental distortion and emotions in an attempt to seize power, control and privileges at the victim's expense. People who manipulate others are usually doing so because they want to avoid being direct about whatever it is that they want. There are a number of different types of manipulation with some being more obvious than others.

In normal communication there is a give and take to constructive results. Manipulation on the other hand benefits one at the expense of the other in order to serve their agenda. Manipulators are good at reading people and detecting their weaknesses. Then they can convince them to give up something or serve them.

This isn't something that happens as a one time event. In fact, more often than not manipulation is an ongoing process of toxic relationships. Once a manipulator has violated someone they are likely to do it again and again until the victim puts a stop to it.

Manipulation consists of three factors, fear, obligation and guilt. The most common manipulators you will encounter are the bully and the victim.

The Bully

The bully uses aggression and intimidation to control you and make you feel fear. For example someone might challenge your insecurities and confidence by making remarks about your abilities or asking you questions that put you in a negative position. Politicians and celebrities are frequently challenged by the media to put them into negative situations. If your wit isn't sharply developed these quick and deadly attacks can make you look bad and in turn lower your social value. However if you are skilled and fast in this art, the attack can be deflected or be counter attacked to boost your social value.

The Victim

The victim uses guilt to manipulate others and make them feel responsible to stop their suffering. Manipulative people might make you feel like you have done something wrong when in reality you probably have not. This makes the manipulated person question themselves or feel a sense of guilt and or defensiveness.

This kind of manipulation can be very subtle. A person might consistently do a lot of favors for people. However with every favor there is always a string attached. Or some kind of expectation. If you don't return the favor you will be made to feel guilty and look ungrateful. This is an exploitation of the expectation of returning favors and is one of the most common ways that people are manipulated.

It's a standard expectation for us to return favors. Even if someone does so insincerely. This is often why some cultures won't accept gifts from strangers. For example, sales people make is seem like they gave you a great deal as a favor. So you should buy their products to return the favor. Or maybe your colleague bought you a coffee and so you better feel obligated to return the favor.

There are two very common manipulation tactics that are used by manipulators.

Foot in the door

The foot in the door tactic involves someone starts with a small and reasonable request.

"Can I take the afternoon off?"
"Do you have a few minutes to talk?"

This will then lead to a much larger request.

"Can I now take the rest of the month off?"
"You just need $100 invested."

Door in the face

The door in the face technique is the opposite. It starts with someone making a big request. This is very likely to get rejected and then they make a much smaller request. For example someone might ask you for a large amount of money up front. Then when you decline it they will request a smaller amount. This will appear much more reasonable in comparison.

Dealing with manipulation

Consider if you are being manipulated. Ask yourself if your being treated with respect and if the persons demands are reasonable or not. Ultimately you should consider if you really feel good about the relationship. How you answer these questions will help you to identify whether or not the relationship has any further value for you.

In addition you can also ask those questions back onto the potentially manipulative person. Ask them if it seems reasonable and fair to them. Or ask what will you get out of this. It is a good idea to restate their requests to them in order to gain clarity. When you do this it will show the other person the nature of their requests. This might trigger them to back down or withdraw demands.

If they persist with demands you can use time as a leverage to distance yourself. Simply say something like "let me think about it". Take your time and evaluate the request. Remember that it is your human right to say no if you want to later on. If you remain passive and compliant this will give strength to the manipulator. When you start to stand up for yourself then they will back down.

The way you respond to manipulation will depend on the kind of manipulation you are facing. If you are in abusive manipulative relationships it is better to seek treatment and advice from a trained therapist. Otherwise you should leave any toxic relationships.

Establishing personal boundaries plays an important role in reducing manipulation. You have the right to stand up for yourself and defend yourself. We all deserve to be treated with respect, to express our feelings, wants and to say no. Regardless of feeling guilty it is your right to live according to your own terms and conditions for happiness. Manipulative people will try to take advantage and deprive you of your rights. But you have the authority to take control of your life.

In a case of a manipulative work life scenario try to delay your responses. Take the time to analyze the situation. Even better if you have a second person with you. Voice that you need time to consider. Avoid making decisions there and then. Sometimes it's better to sleep on it. Appearing unintelligent will act as a concealment. Try to think in a logical way and take your emotions out of the decisions.

Always be reading and analyzing people to identify potentially manipulative people. Observe how they behave in different situations and with different people. Of course we all act differently in various situations but manipulative people tend to be more extreme in their behavioural differences. In some cases they could be perfectly polite whilst in others they are harsh and rude. If you notice this kind of erratic behavior do not to get involved with them. Reasons for manipulative behavior can be complex psychological issues that need to be dealt with by experts.

Finally, remember that manipulating people for your own selfish goals will not bring you true happiness. Yes, it can easily make you a rich and powerful person but if you don't have anyone that cares about you who you can be truthful with then you will be forever alone.

Conclusion

Here we are. The way you see people will never be the same. Day to day life will be more of an adventure as you observe the various types of people you come across. Your social circle will widen as you begin to read and understand people better. Predicting the behaviour of people even if you just met them will come to you much more easily. You will probably find that your personal and professional relationships will change dramatically for the better. All of this will lead to a better life in harmony with people around you.

It might be time to move on from certain relationships that you have identified as not adding value to you anymore. Living your best life depends on this. You can know that it is the right choice. You can't change people if they don't want to change but you have the power to walk away. To walk away to better things and open new doors in your life.

Trust yourself when you read people. Voices, faces and bodies don't lie. Your intuition is closest to the truth. With this powerful understanding of reading people you are armed with a greater self awareness, more empathy and social confidence. You will be able to see what is true and what is not.

You need to have a trained and sharp mind in order to understand the words and actions of people on multiple levels. Communication is a multi layered form of conveying messages. You need to be aware of what is really meant and implied. This is a skill that can be practiced and improved upon by analyzing and interacting with the people around you. Take notice of the words people use, observe their body language, try to figure out their values and what it is that drives them. Poker players are masters of this skill. Having the ability to identify who is bluffing and who is not.

Whilst you read people make sure you read yourself objectively. Examine your posture, tonality and how you come across. You always want to be presenting the best version of yourself. Observe how people react to you and ask them for feedback. Good friends will be happy to give you honest feedback if you tell them that you are trying to improve.

All this helps to have successful interactions and to be judged more positively. After your interactions ask yourself, what went well, what didn't and what you can improve upon. Keep a journal of your progress and highlight the things you need to work on. Maybe you need a course on tonality or you could benefit from yoga for your posture or acting classes for expressing yourself and so on. Be self aware and journal to really track that and then excel.

Social intelligence and reading people increases your health. The more socially connected we are the more happy we feel. As a direct result our health improves.

In turn, the better we can become at reading people the more opportunity it will bring us.

This book is not intended to make you a master manipulator that takes advantage of people. Rather it is a way to help you read people and have better interactions. This will help you make better decisions, increase your happiness and improve your relationships. Use the information in this book to help you live your best life.

Power is in the people.

Thanks for Reading!

What did you think of, **Magnetic: How Anyone Can Learn Genuine Charisma, Confidence, Body Language, & People Reading Skills Without Being Weird, Needy Or Arrogant**

I know you could have picked any number of books to read, but you picked this book and for that I am extremely grateful.

I hope that it added at value and quality to your everyday life. If so, it would be really nice if you could share this book with your friends and family by posting to **Facebook** and **Twitter**.

If you enjoyed this book and found some benefit in reading this, I'd like to hear from you and hope that you could take some time to post a review.

Your feedback and support will help me to greatly improve for future projects and make this book even better.

I wish you all the best in your future success!

Darcy Carter

Buyer Bonus:

Rituals Of The Rich & Famous

Free Access to Success Tips, Strategies and Habits of The Rich & Famous

Join successful subscribers!

Get 4 new strategies every week on how to be more charismatic, confident, and happy.

<u>Free Sign Up Here</u>

Buyer Bonus 2

<u>Attachment Theory, The Science of Successful Relationships, Authentic Love, Romance and Connection</u>

Discover the secrets to building healthy, happy, and rewarding relationships.

The key ingredient to happy and fulfilled people is the quality of their intimate, social, family, and professional relationships - nothing else in life comes even remotely close.

Go ahead, transform the quality of your relationships and make love work for you.

ATTACHMENT THEORY

The Science of Successful Relationships, Authentic Love, Romance and Connection

DARCY CARTER

www.ingramcontent.com/pod-product-compliance
Lightning Source LLC
Chambersburg PA
CBHW030245030426
42336CB00009B/265